S.N.C.C.

SMALL PROJECTS FOR SMALL HANDS
Arts & Crafts For Beginning Skills Concepts

S.N.C.C.

written and illustrated by Lynn Brisson

Incentive Publications, Inc.
Nashville, Tennessee

Cover design by Angela C. Wilson
Edited by Sherri Y. Lewis

ISBN 0-86530-187-5

© 1991 by Incentive Publications, Inc., Nashville, TN. No part of this publication may be reproduced, stored in a retrieval system, or transmitted in any form or by any means (electronic, mechanical, photocopying, recording, or otherwise) without prior written permission from Incentive Publications, Inc., with the exception below.

Pages labeled with the statement © 1991 by Incentive Publications, Inc., Nashville, TN are intended for reproduction. Permission is hereby granted to the purchaser of one copy of SMALL PROJECTS FOR SMALL HANDS to reproduce, in sufficient quantities for meeting yearly classroom needs.

TABLE OF CONTENTS

Introduction..6
Mailbox..7
Pretty Parrot...10
Tabletop Telephone...13
Barn..16
Gingerbread Man..19
Alphabet Turtle...21
Open House Invitation 24
Counting Caterpillar 27
Big Whale 29
Days Of The Week 32
Name Tag And Award Necklaces 35
Birthday Banner..38
Finger Puppet Pets...40
Dinosaur Display..42
Sammy Seal Balances Shapes 45
Certificates 50
Jack-In-The-Box...55
Colored Crayons 58
Good Dental Habits..61
Helper Bees 62
Humpty-Dumpty..66
Weather Bear 69
Happy Hen..71
Roaring Good Time 73
Ladybug..76
Beautiful Butterfly 78

INTRODUCTION

SMALL PROJECTS FOR SMALL HANDS is the easy activity book you have been looking for to help young children master beginning skills and concepts.

Chock-full of simple, fun paper projects, SMALL PROJECTS FOR SMALL HANDS incorporates learning with play. Children learn how to count with a caterpillar, say their "A, B, Cs" with a turtle, and learn how to dial their phone number on a play phone.

Easy-to-follow instructions, no-fuss materials needed, and a use for each activity make this primary source an asset to your simple projects library.

MAILBOX

MATERIALS:
- construction paper
- crayons
- brads
- paste
- scissors

CONSTRUCTION:
1. Reproduce the patterns.
2. Color and cut out the patterns.
3. Cut along dotted lines.
4. Insert brad through the flag and attach to the mailbox.
5. Turn mailbox pattern over and place paste between the arrows as shown on pattern. Fold the pattern back. (Do not place paste around the opening of the mailbox.)
6. Paste post to the mailbox.
7. Have the students write their addresses on the mailboxes.

USE:
Paste the mailbox to a piece of construction paper or attach to a bulletin board. This activity will help the students remember their addresses. It can also be used for special deliveries such as notes to take home or homework reminders.

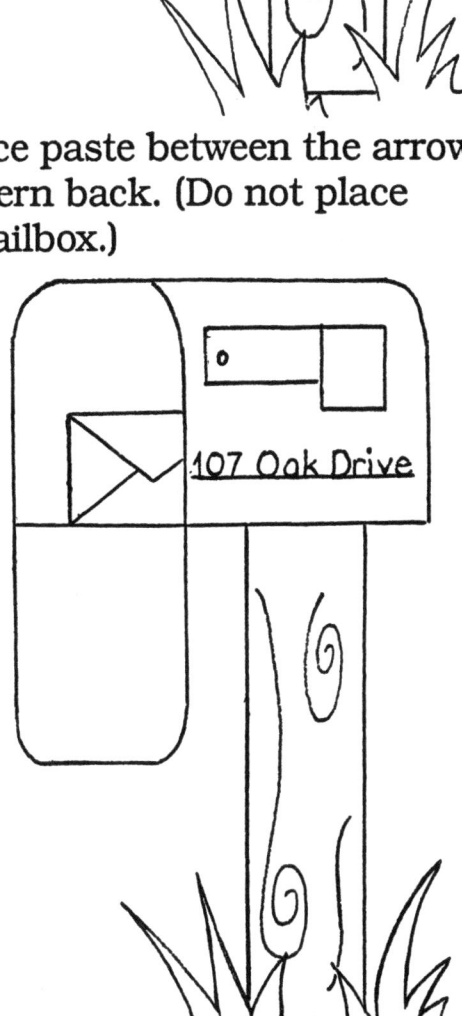

7

MAILBOX PATTERN

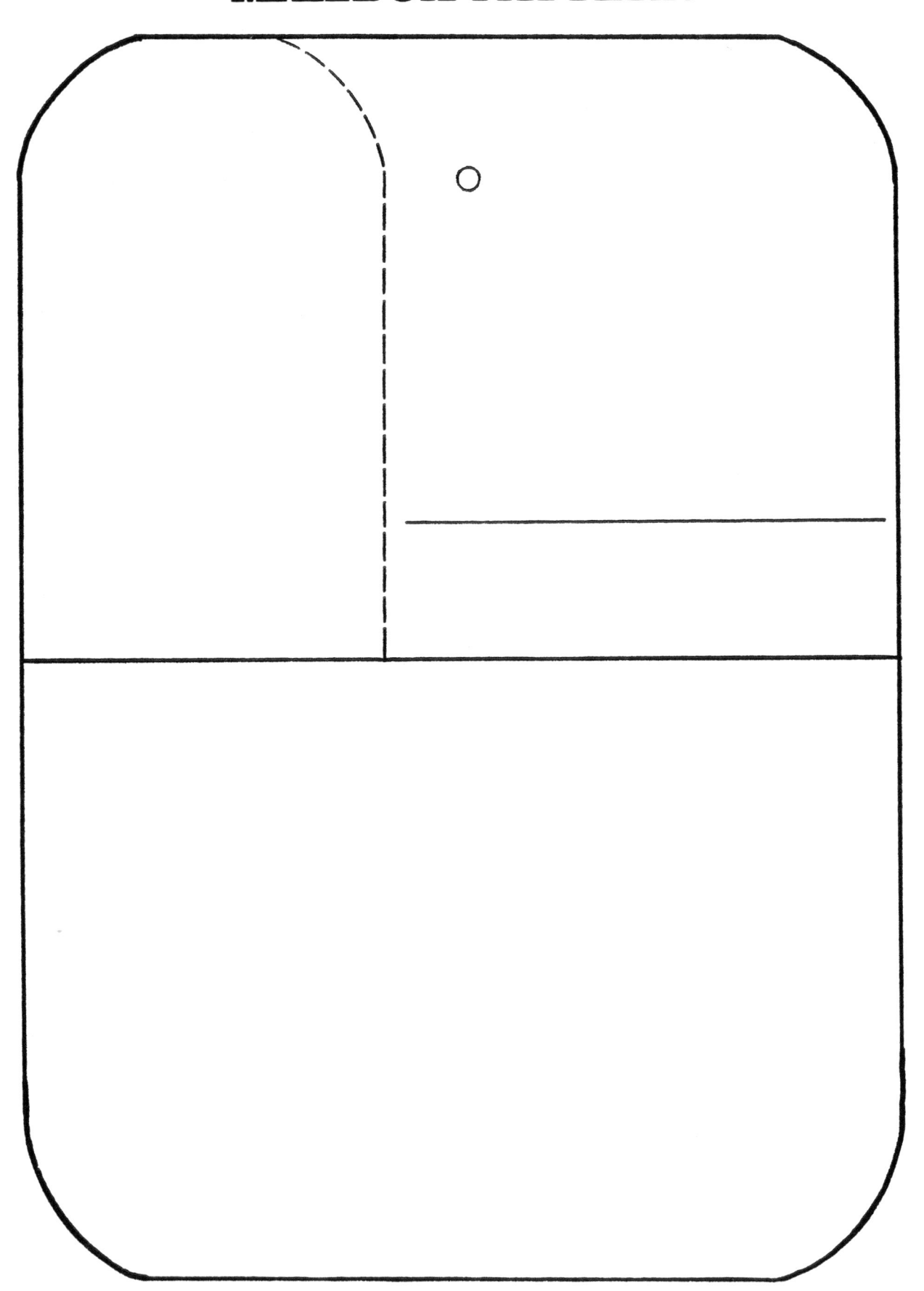

MAILBOX PATTERN

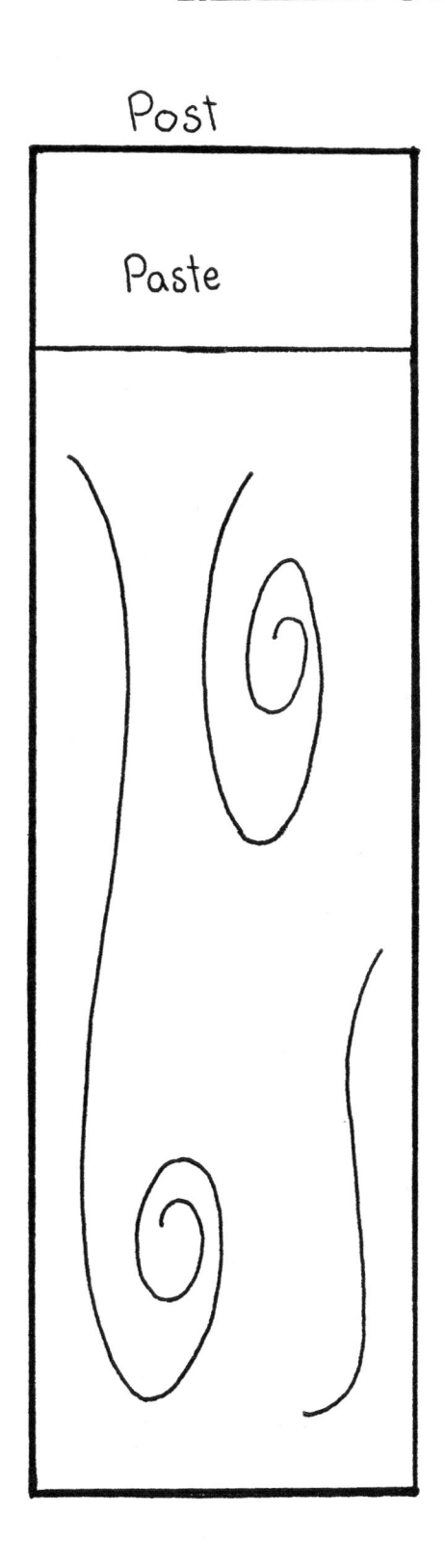

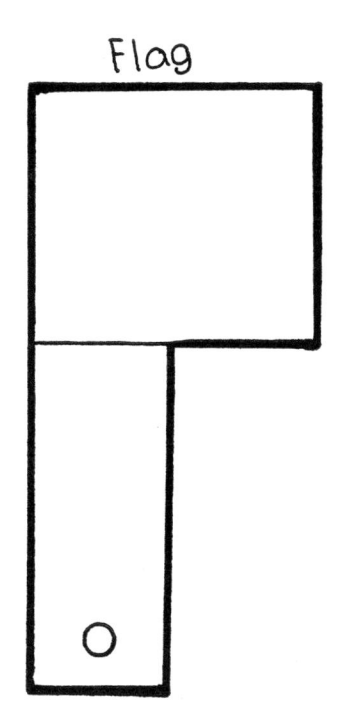

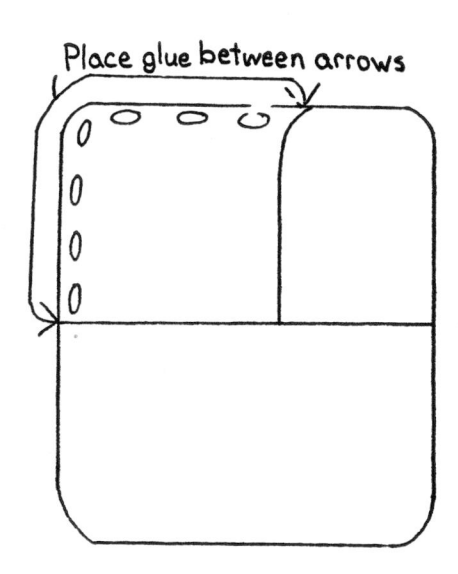

Post

Paste

Flag

Place glue between arrows

© 1991 by Incentive Publications, Inc., Nashville, TN.

PRETTY PARROT

MATERIALS:
- construction paper
- hole punch
- yarn
- paste
- scissors
- crayons

CONSTRUCTION:
1. Reproduce the patterns.
2. Color and cut out the patterns.
3. Paste parrot to the cage.
4. Punch a hole in the top of the cage, place yarn through the hole, and tie.

USE:
Hang the students' colorful parrots in the classroom for decoration.

PARROT PATTERN

CAGE PATTERN

TABLETOP TELEPHONE

MATERIALS:
- construction paper
- yarn
- hole punch
- crayons
- paste
- scissors

CONSTRUCTION:
1. Reproduce the patterns.
2. Color and cut out the patterns.
3. Have each student write his/her telephone number on the telephone.
4. Punch holes in the telephone and receiver.
5. Cut along the dotted lines.
6. Fold the front and back of the telephone pattern up along the straight lines.
7. Place paste across the top of the telephone; then paste the two sides together. This will create a stand-up telephone.
8. Tie a piece of yarn to the telephone and receiver. Place the receiver in the slits.

USE:
This activity will help the students learn their telephone numbers when playing with their telephones.

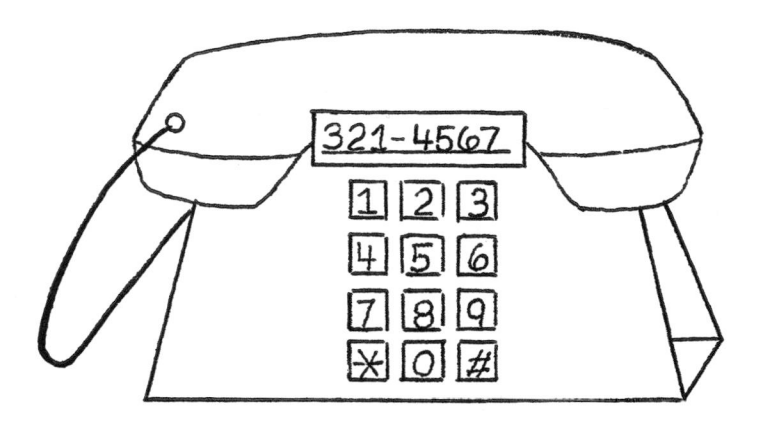

TELEPHONE RECEIVER PATTERN

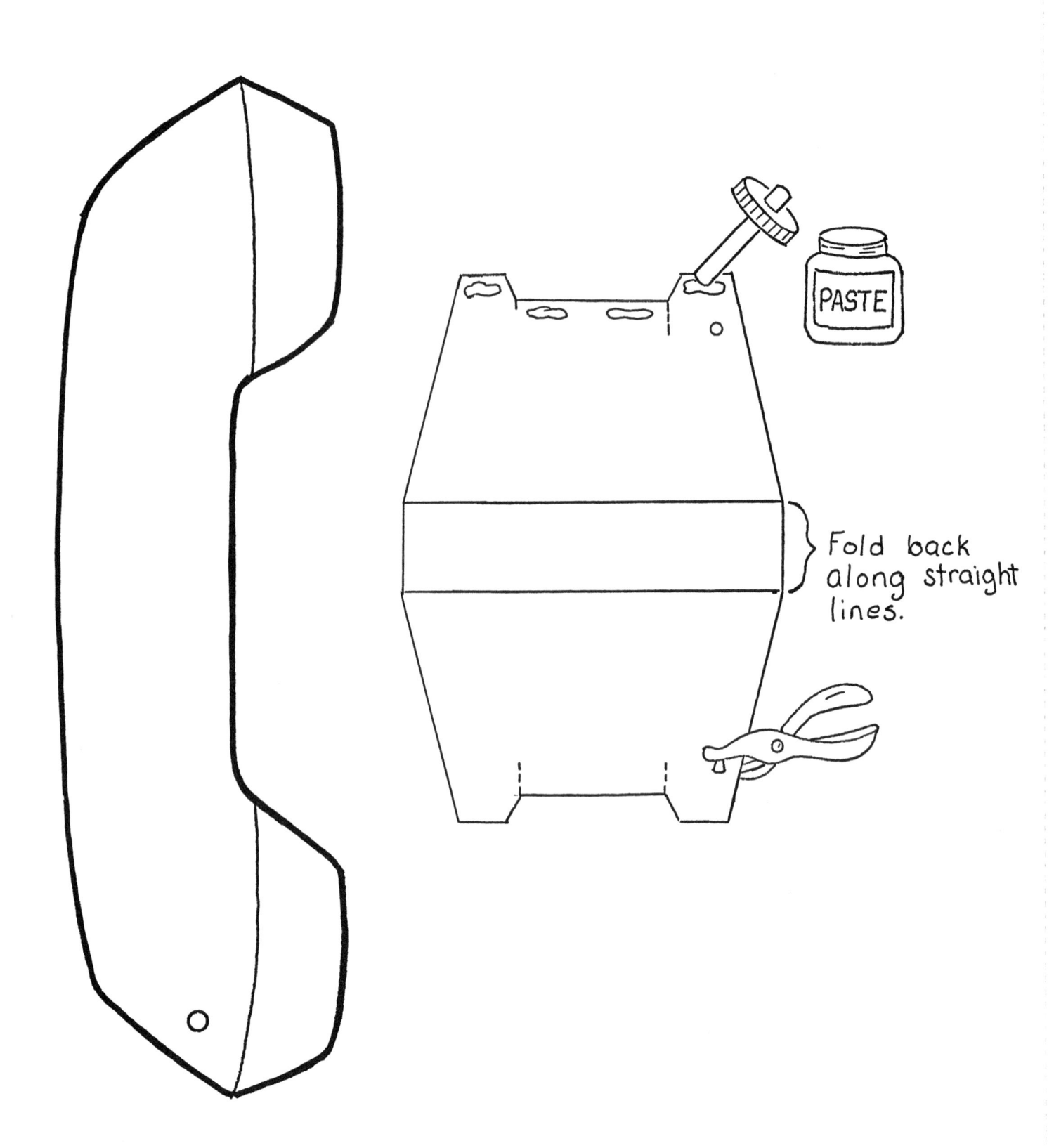

Fold back along straight lines.

TELEPHONE PATTERN

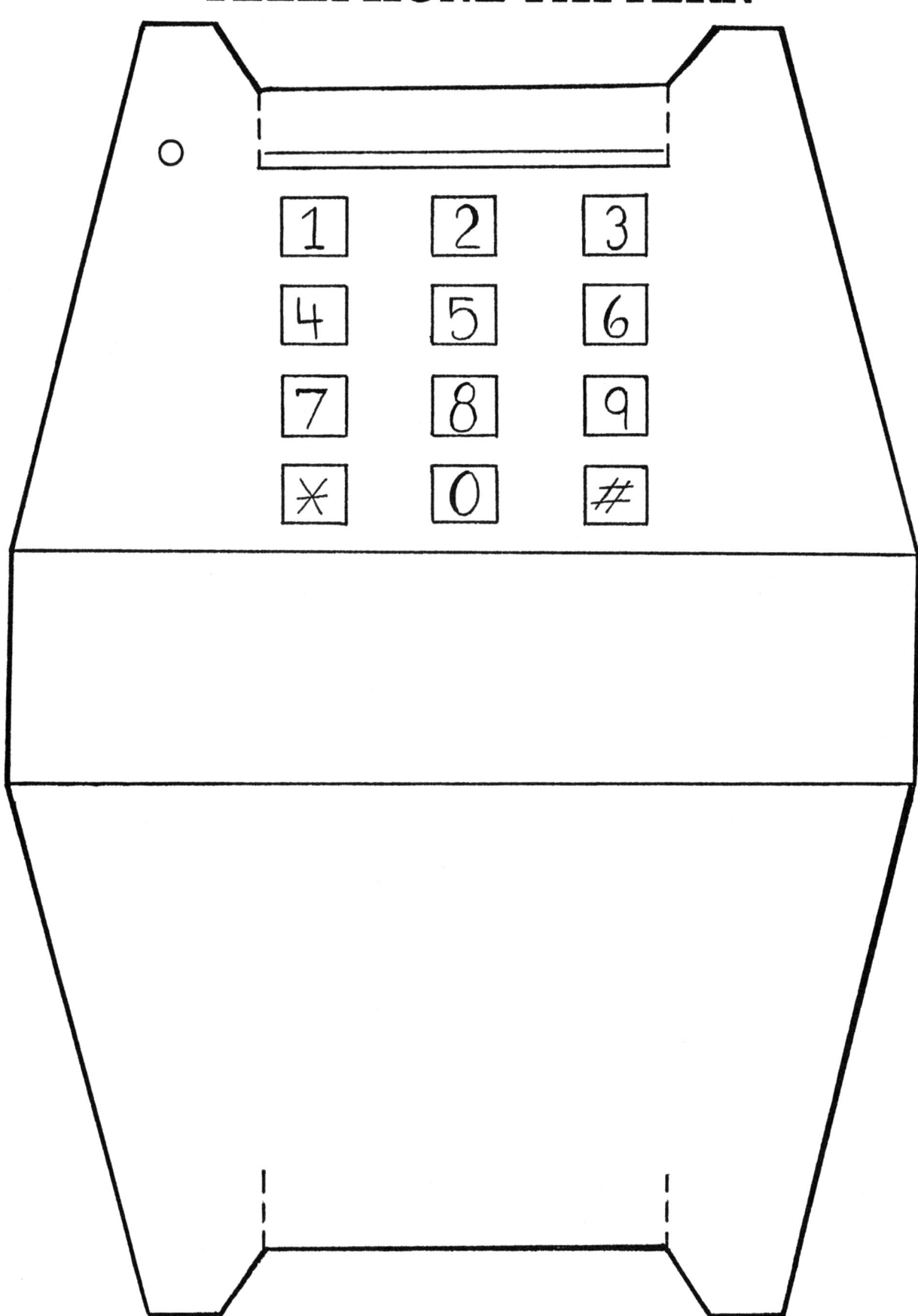

© 1991 by Incentive Publications, Inc., Nashville, TN.

BARN

MATERIALS:
- construction paper
- crayons
- paste
- scissors

CONSTRUCTION:
1. Reproduce and cut out the patterns.
2. Fold the door pattern along the dotted lines; then paste to the barn. Paste on the silo.
3. Draw farm animals inside the door and windows.
4. Color the animals and barn with crayons.

USE:
Talk to the students about different kinds of animals found on a farm. Have the students draw their favorite animals in the barns. Read *The Big Red Barn* by Margaret Wise Brown to the students.

BARN PATTERN

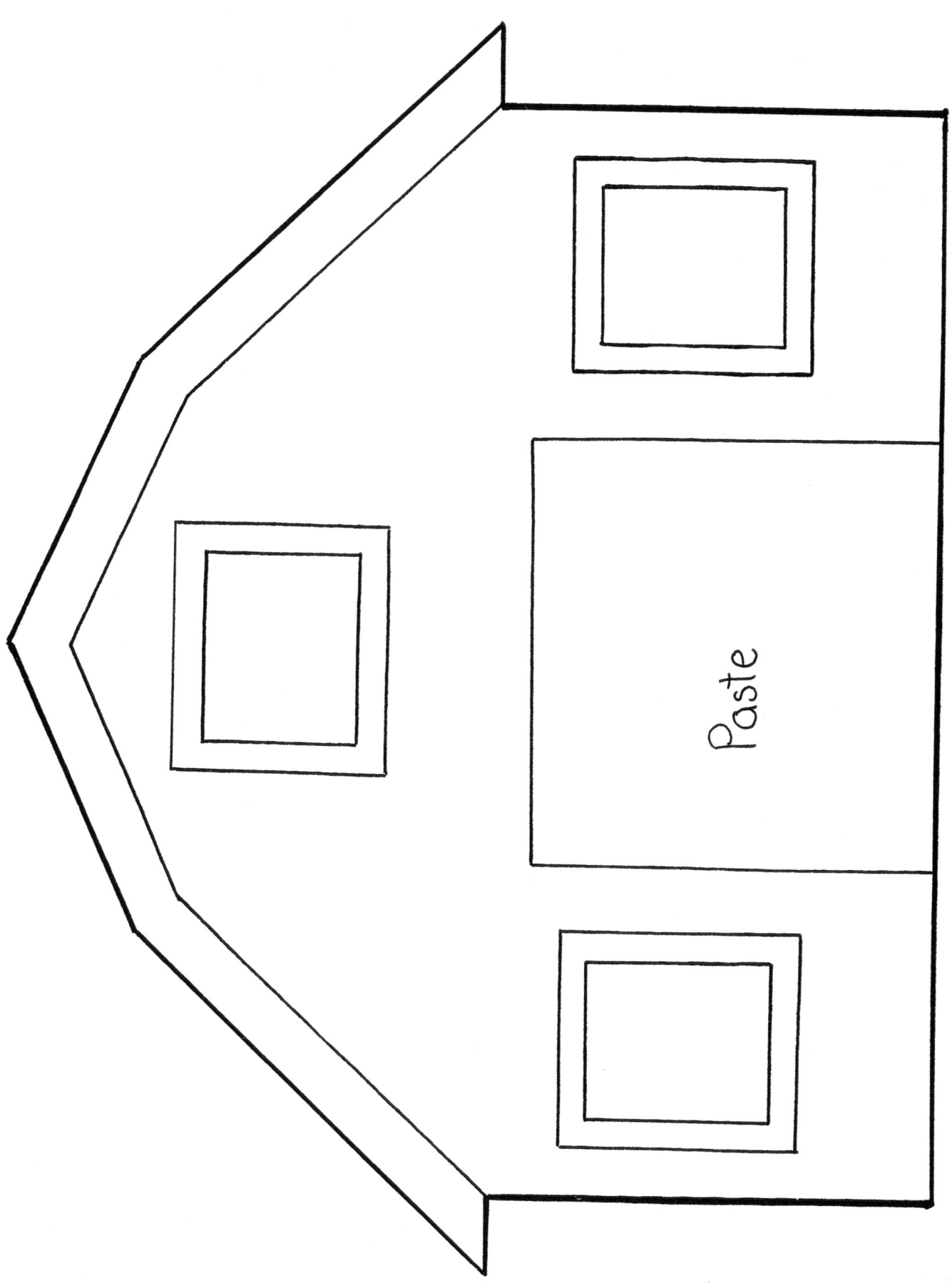

Paste

SILO PATTERN

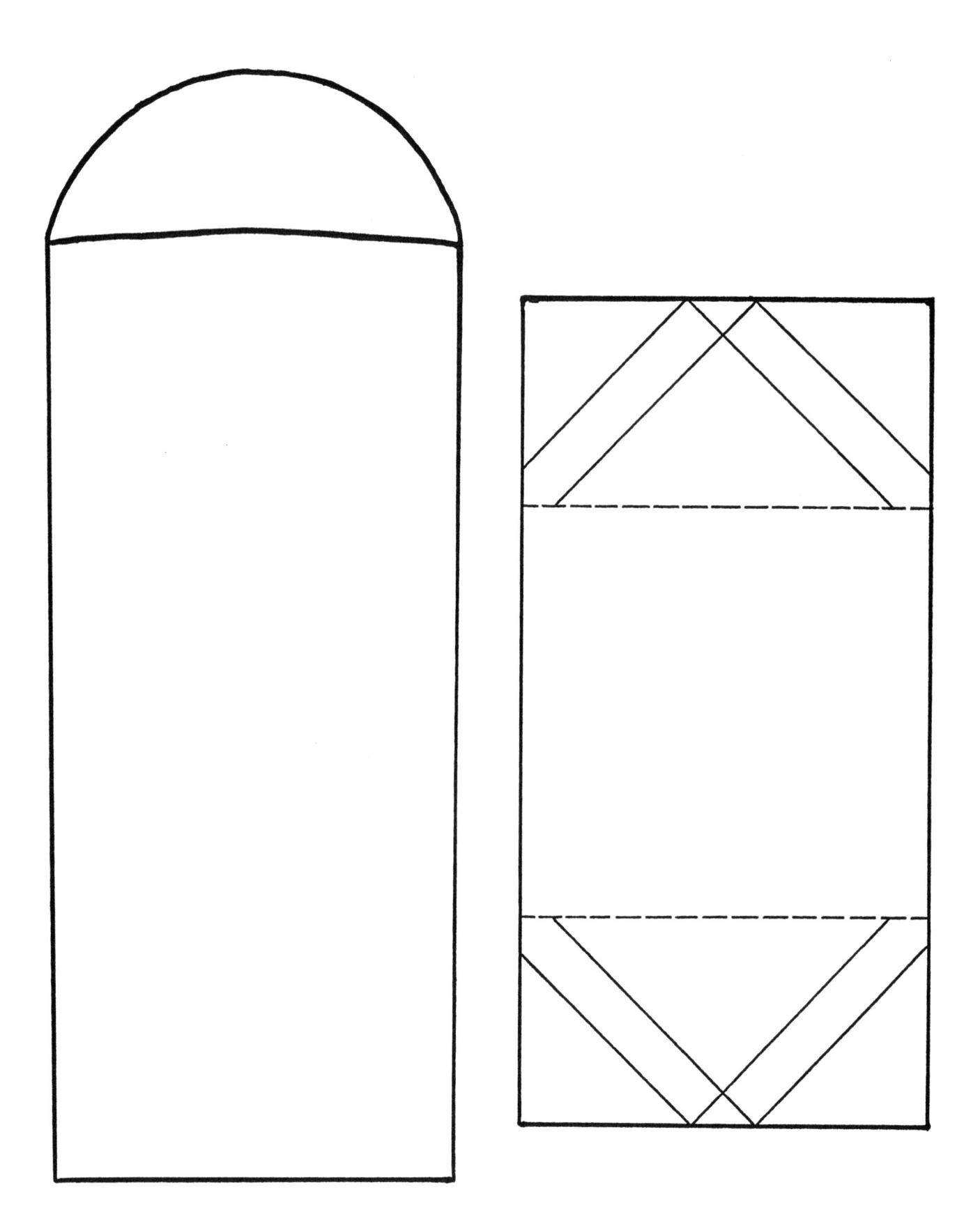

GINGERBREAD MAN

MATERIALS:
- construction paper
- crayons
- uncooked macaroni
- paste
- scissors

CONSTRUCTION:
1. Reproduce the pattern.
2. Color and cut out the pattern.
3. Paste macaroni around the gingerbread man.

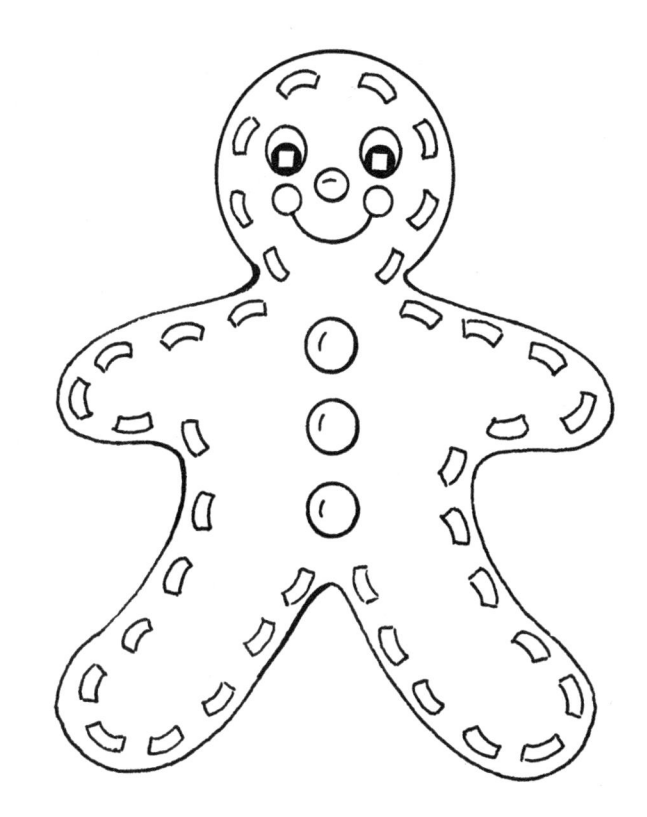

USE:

Read *The Gingerbread Man* to the students. Let them make a gingerbread man for the bulletin board. Students will enjoy making gingerbread men for Christmas decorations. They can be used to decorate the classroom or to take home.

GINGERBREAD MAN PATTERN

ALPHABET TURTLE

MATERIALS:
- construction paper
- crayons
- paste
- scissors

CONSTRUCTION:
1. Reproduce the patterns.
2. Have the students write the alphabet on the turtle.
3. Color and cut out the patterns.
4. Cut along the dotted lines. This will create grass.
5. Place paste on each side of the pattern; then fold back along the straight line. This will form a pocket.
6. Place turtle in the pocket.

USE:
The students will enjoy writing the alphabet when they get to write it on the turtle's shell.

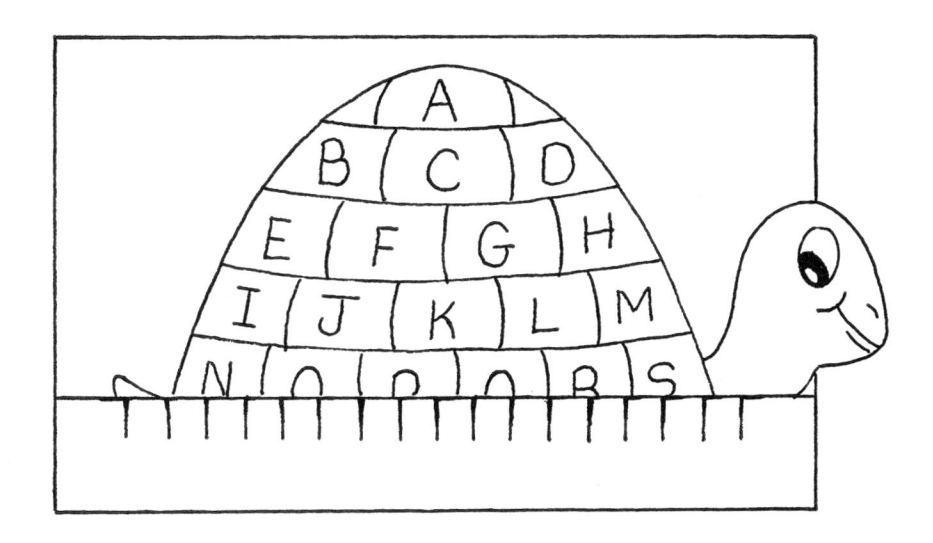

TURTLE PATTERN

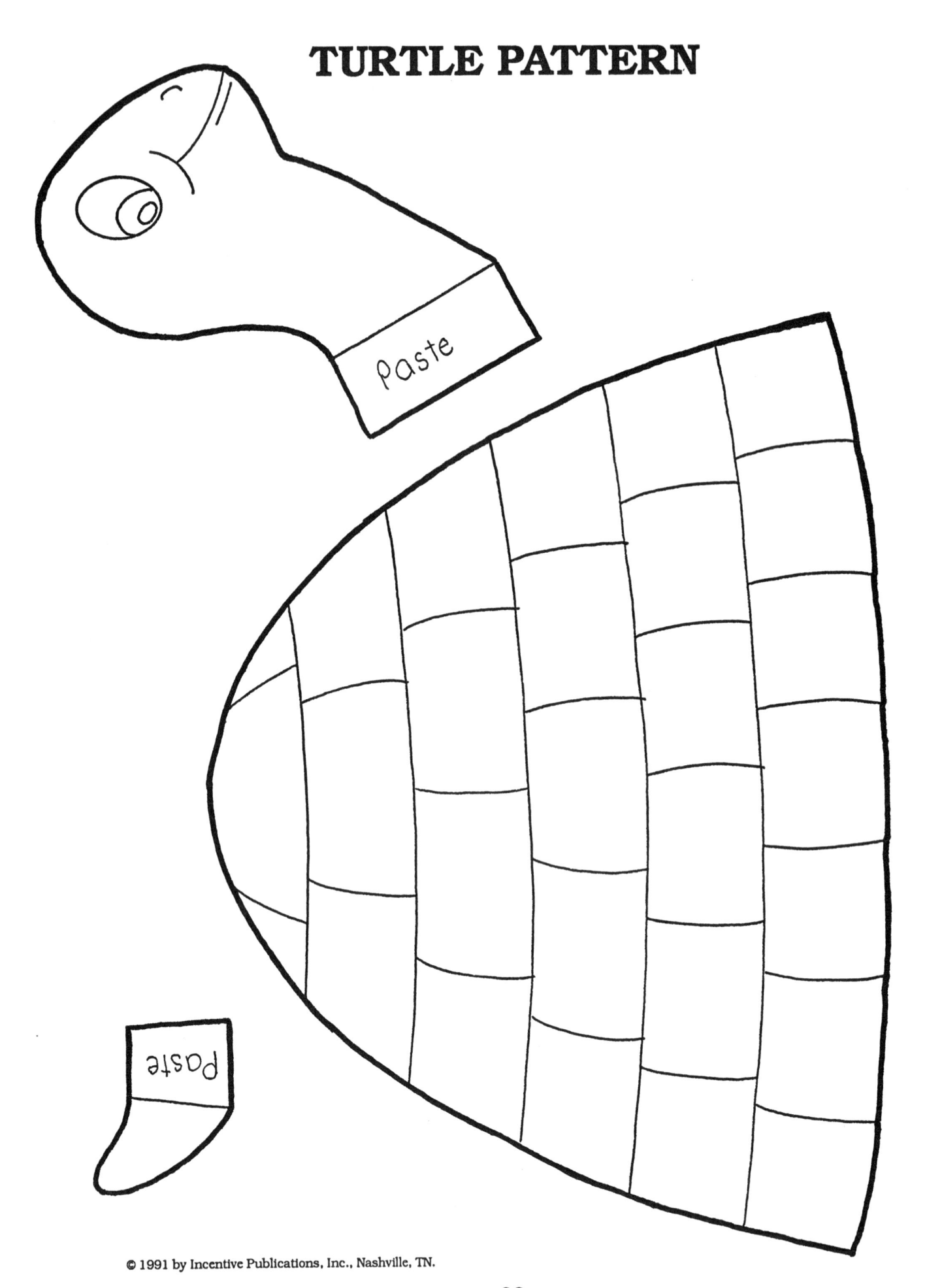

Paste

Paste

© 1991 by Incentive Publications, Inc., Nashville, TN.

BACKGROUND PATTERN

OPEN HOUSE INVITATION

MATERIALS:
- construction paper
- crayons
- paste
- scissors

CONSTRUCTION:
1. Reproduce the patterns.
2. Color and cut out the patterns.
3. Cut pattern along the dotted lines.
4. Crumple the strips of cut paper with your hand. This will add dimension to the nest.
5. Paste the branches to a piece of construction paper; then paste the bird to the bottom branch.

USE:

Use this activity for an open house invitation. Write "Open House" on the top branch and the information about the open house on the bottom half of the construction paper. This activity can be used in the spring to brighten up the classroom. Attach the birds and branches to a bulletin board covered with blue paper and trimmed with a yellow border.

BIRD PATTERN

BRANCHES PATTERN

OPEN HOUSE

Paste

COUNTING CATERPILLAR

MATERIALS:
- construction paper
- crayons
- pencil
- scissors

CONSTRUCTION:
1. Reproduce the patterns.
2. Trace each number with a pencil; then color the patterns.
3. Cut out the patterns and cut along the dotted lines.
4. Fold pattern back along the straight lines to form a stand-up activity.
5. Insert caterpillar pattern in slits.

USE:
This activity will reinforce writing numerals. Read *The Very Hungry Caterpillar* by Eric Carle to the students.

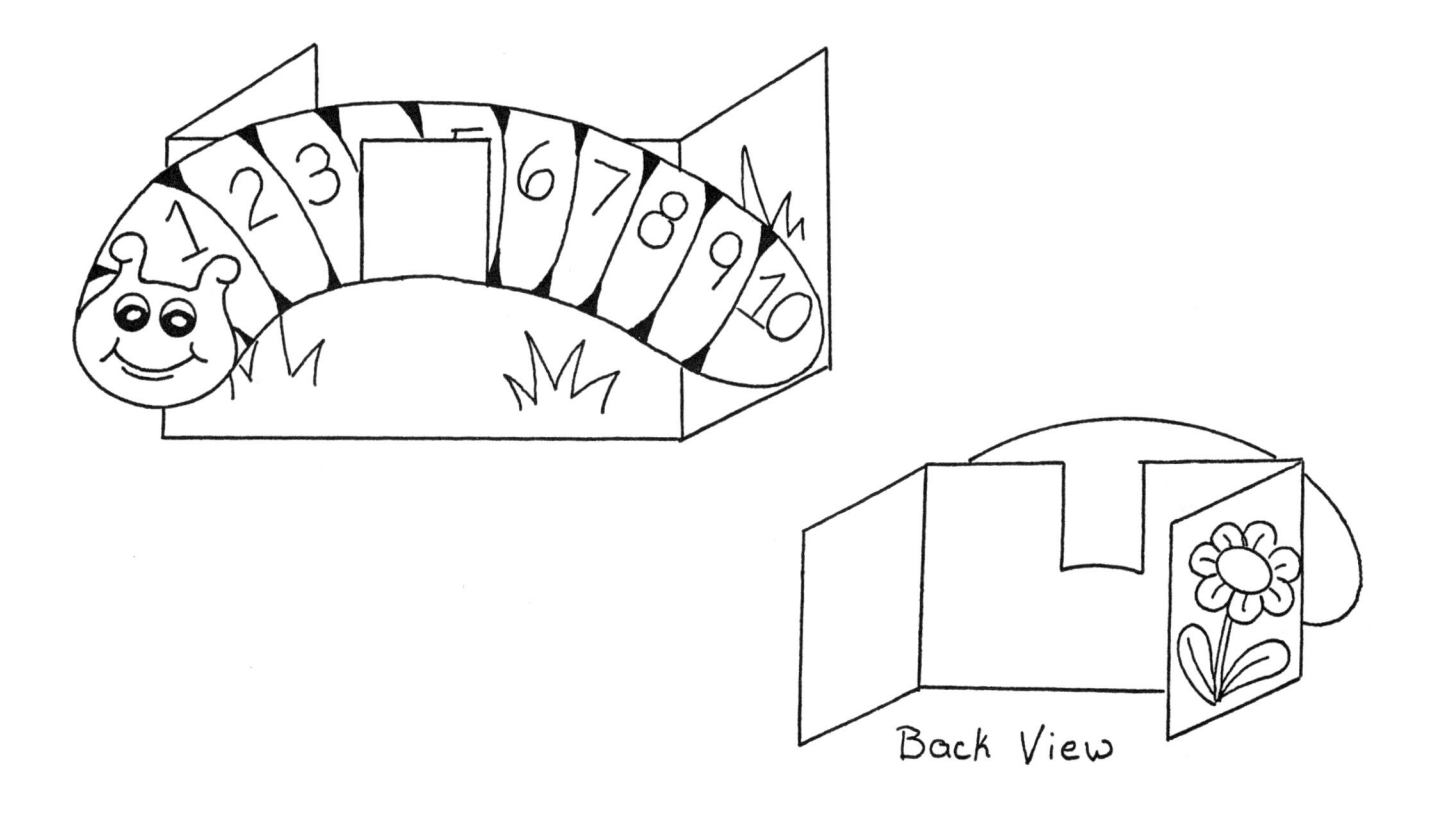

Back View

CATERPILLAR PATTERN

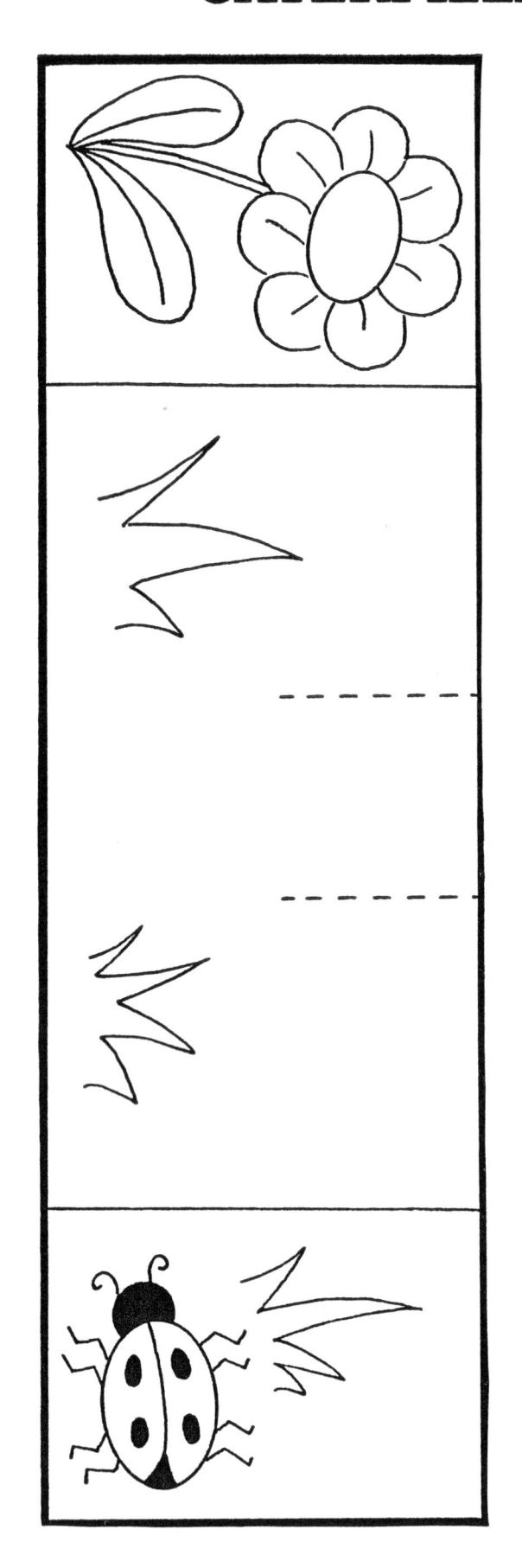

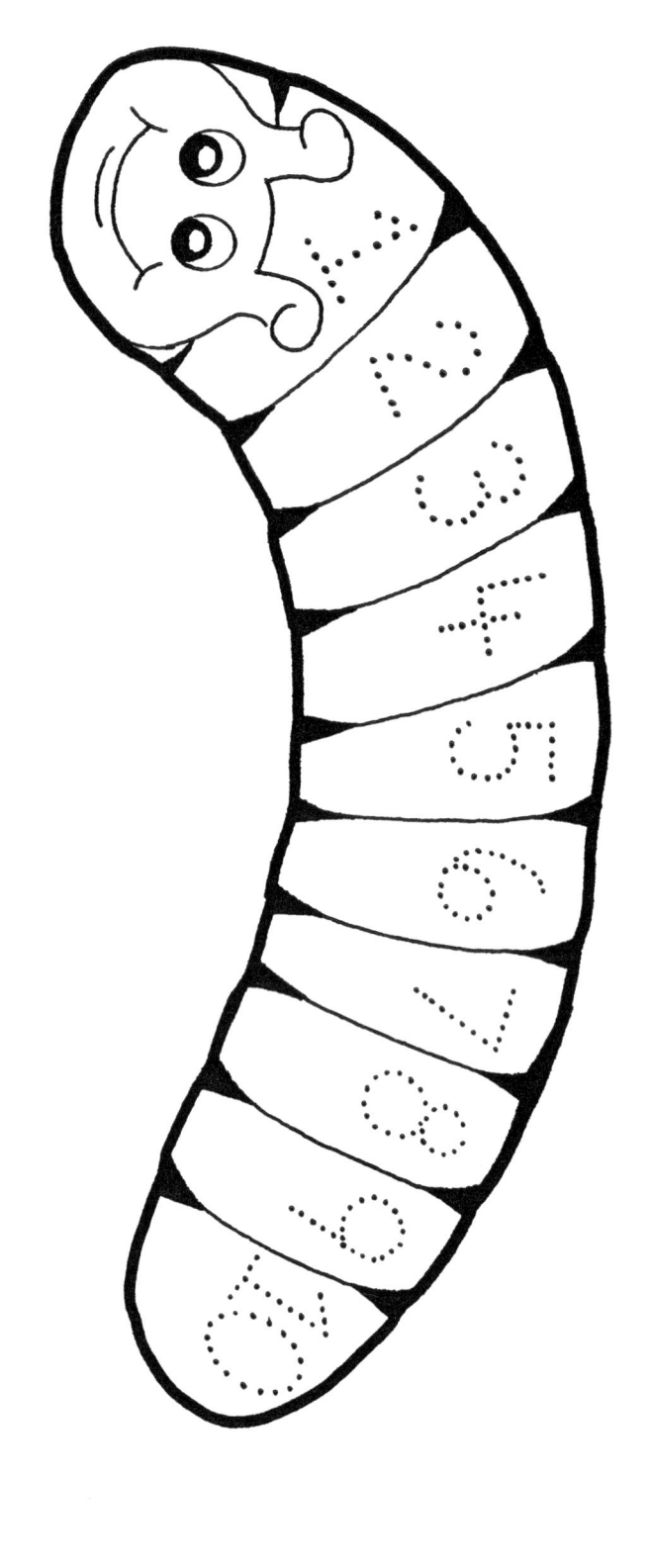

© 1991 by Incentive Publications, Inc., Nashville, TN.

BIG WHALE

MATERIALS:
- construction paper
- crayons
- paste
- scissors

CONSTRUCTION:
1. Reproduce the patterns.
2. Color and cut out the patterns.
3. Place paste on each side of the ocean pattern; then fold back along the dotted lines. This will form a pocket.

USE:
This activity will help the students learn the concept of big and small.

WHALE & FISH PATTERNS

Big

Small

© 1991 by Incentive Publications, Inc., Nashville, TN.

OCEAN PATTERN

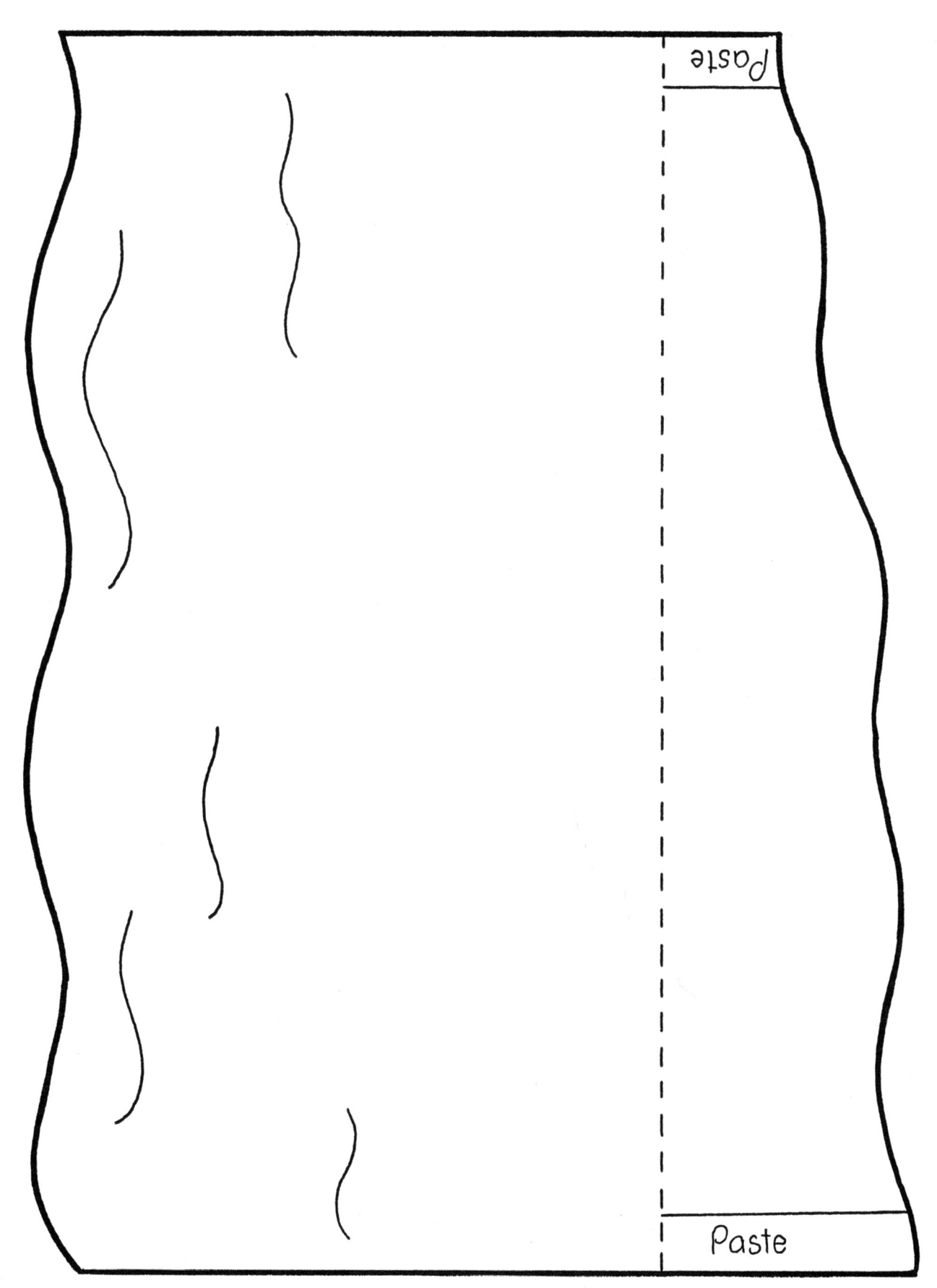

Paste

Paste

© 1991 by Incentive Publications, Inc., Nashville, TN.

DAYS OF THE WEEK

MATERIALS:
- construction paper
- crayons
- brads
- scissors

CONSTRUCTION:
1. Reproduce the patterns.
2. Color and cut out the patterns.
3. Insert brad through center of the wheel and attach it to the circle pattern with the mouse at the top.
4. Turn the wheel each day to the correct day of the week.

USE:
This activity will reinforce the days of the week. Let the students take this activity home for display.

MOUSE/WHEEL PATTERN

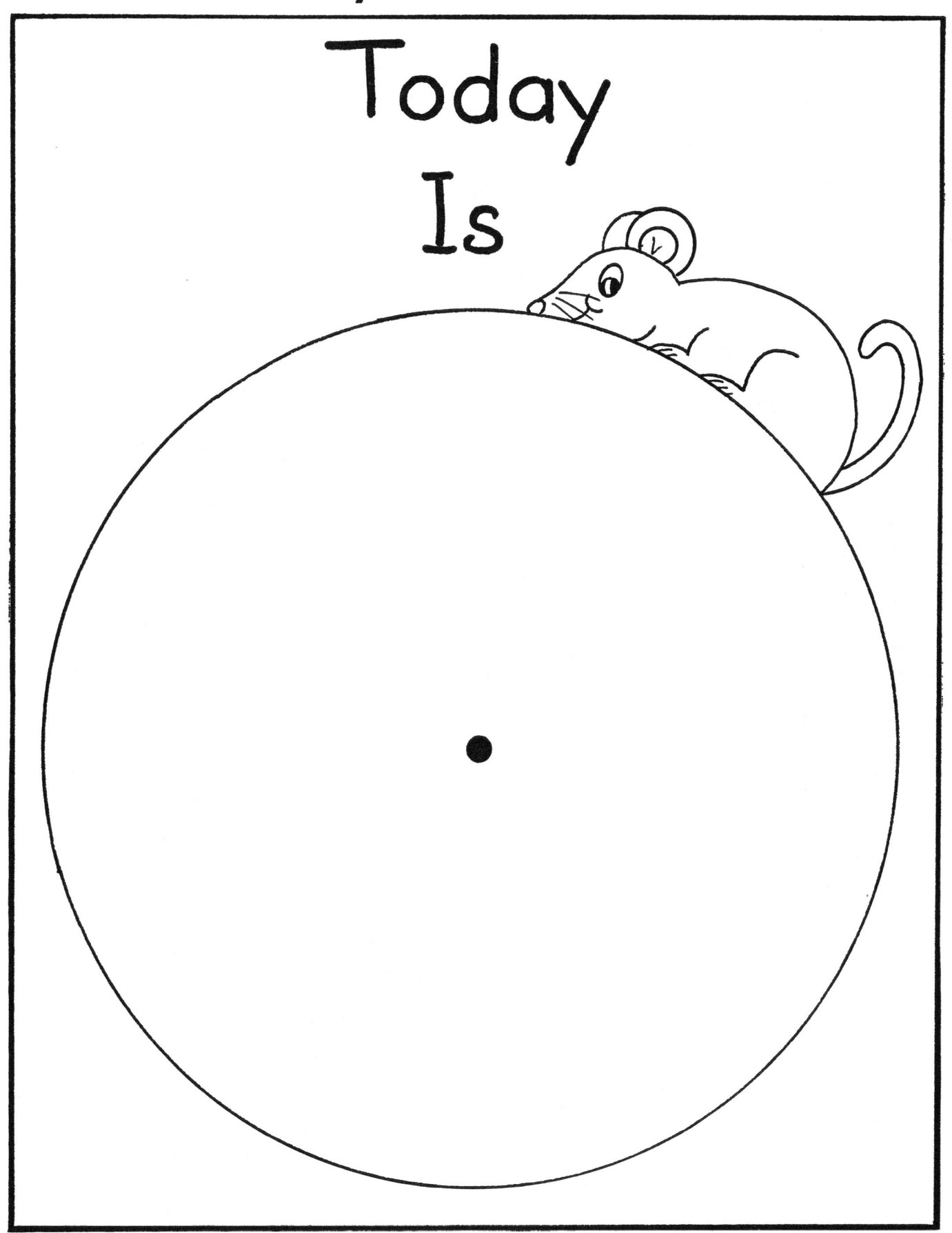

Today Is

© 1991 by Incentive Publications, Inc., Nashville, TN.

WHEEL PATTERN

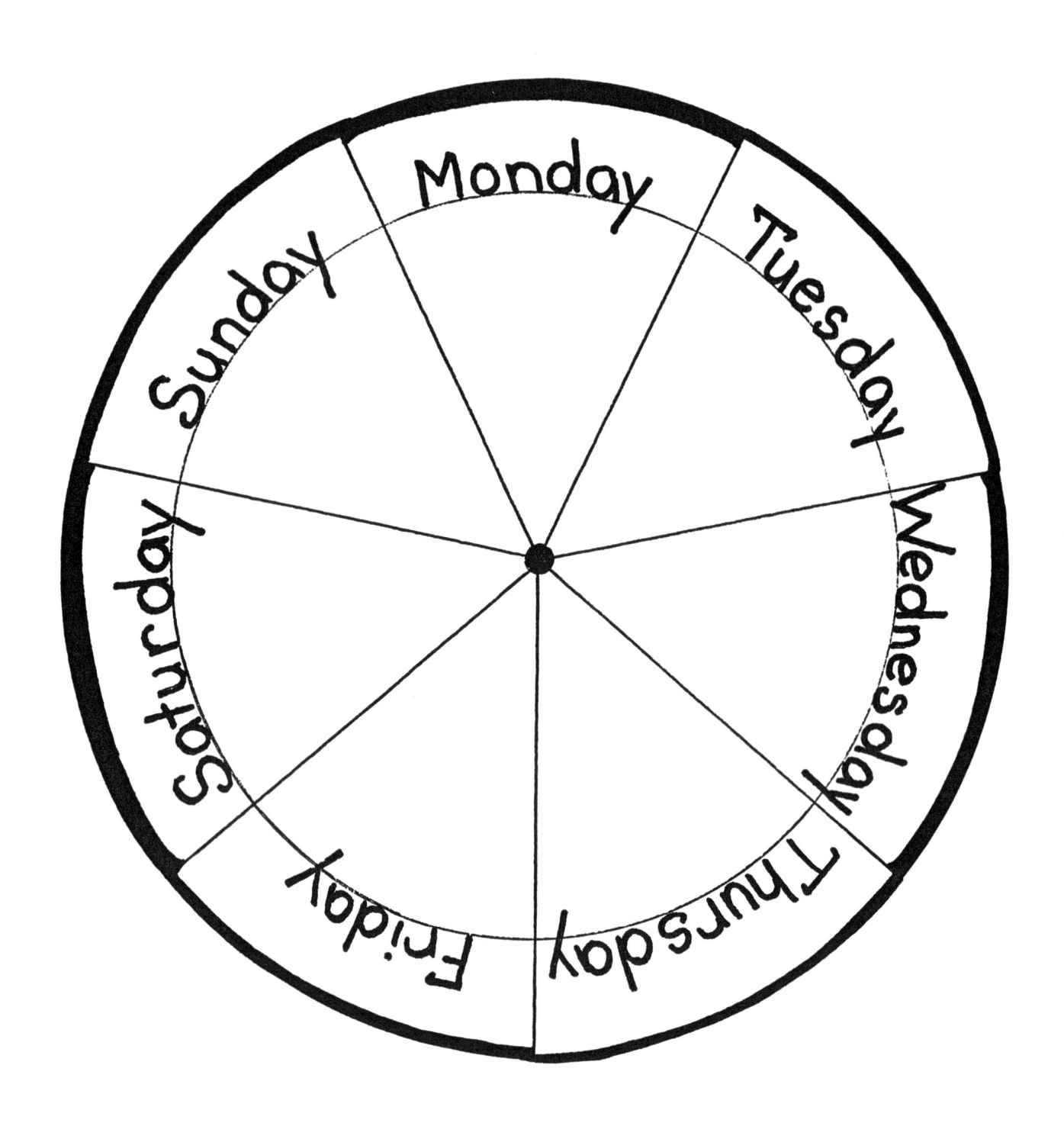

34

NAME TAG AND AWARD NECKLACES

MATERIALS:
- construction paper
- yarn
- crayons
- paste
- scissors

CONSTRUCTION:
1. Reproduce the pattern.
2. Color and cut out pattern.
3. Fold back the tab, place yarn under the tab, and then paste.
4. Tie yarn with a bow.

USE:

On the first day of school, let the students make apple name tag necklaces. Have the students write their names on the apples. This will help the teacher and the students learn names.

Use the other award necklaces for achievements well-done. A specific subject accomplished can be written on the flower necklace (alphabet, colors, address, telephone number, counting, shapes, days of the week, and other subjects).

Students will like wearing award necklaces.

35

AWARD PATTERNS

Back View

My Name Is
_____

Work Well Done

AWARD PATTERNS

I Know My ____

Star Student!

BIRTHDAY BANNER

MATERIALS:
- construction paper
- yarn
- crayons
- paste
- scissors

CONSTRUCTION:
1. Reproduce and write each student's name on a pattern.
2. Let the students color and cut out the banners.
3. Cut along the dotted lines to create the fringe.
4. Fold the top of the pattern back along the straight line. Place a 36 inch piece of yarn under the fold; then paste.
5. Tie yarn with a bow to form a hanging loop.

USE:

Display the banner on each student's birthday.

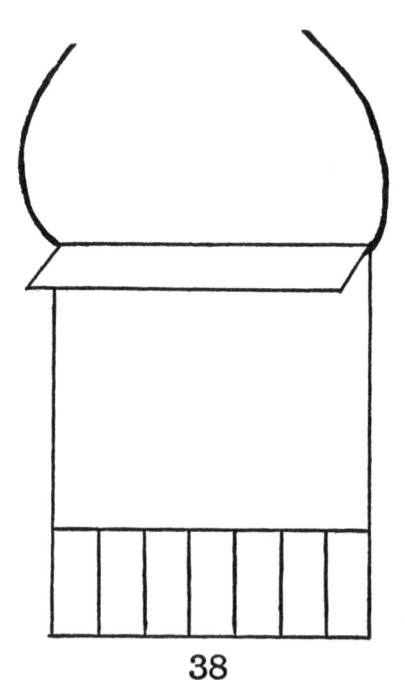

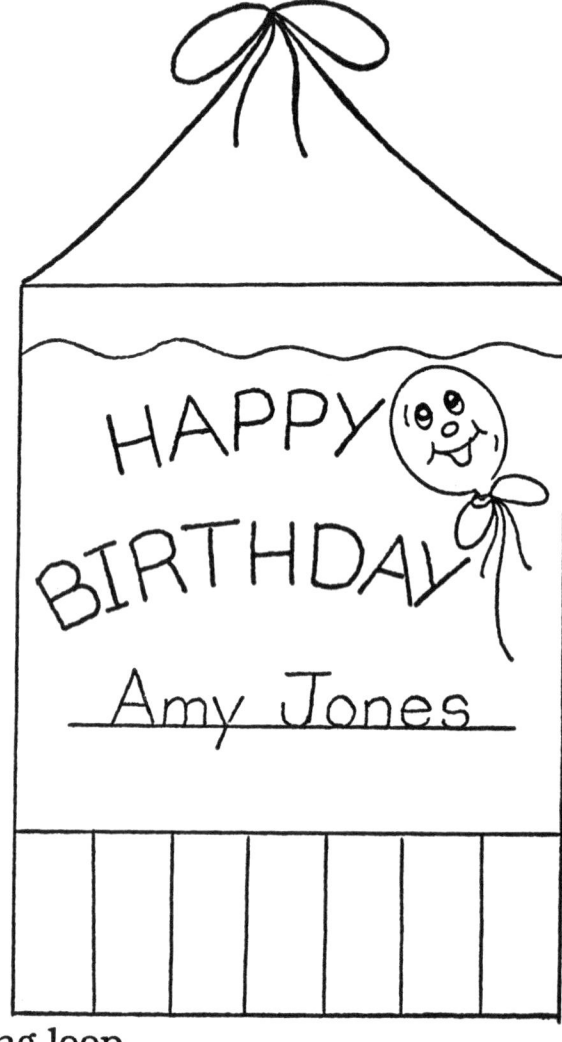

BIRTHDAY PATTERN

Fold Back Along This Line

HAPPY BIRTHDAY

© 1991 by Incentive Publications, Inc., Nashville, TN.

FINGER PUPPET PETS

MATERIALS:
- construction paper
- crayons
- paste
- scissors

CONSTRUCTION:
1. Reproduce the patterns.
2. Color and cut out the patterns.
3. Fold the ears forward along the straight lines and color.
4. Cut along the dotted lines. Fold tabs back and paste.
5. Place fingers through the tabs.

USE:

Use "Spot the dog" and "Katie the cat" for a puppet show. Encourage the students to use their imaginations when playing with the puppets.

Books to read:
Spot Goes To School
Spot Goes To The Circus
Spot Goes To The Beach (all by Eric Hill)

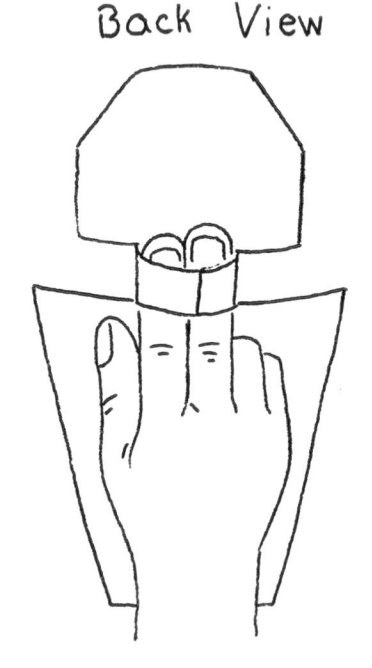

DOG AND CAT PATTERNS

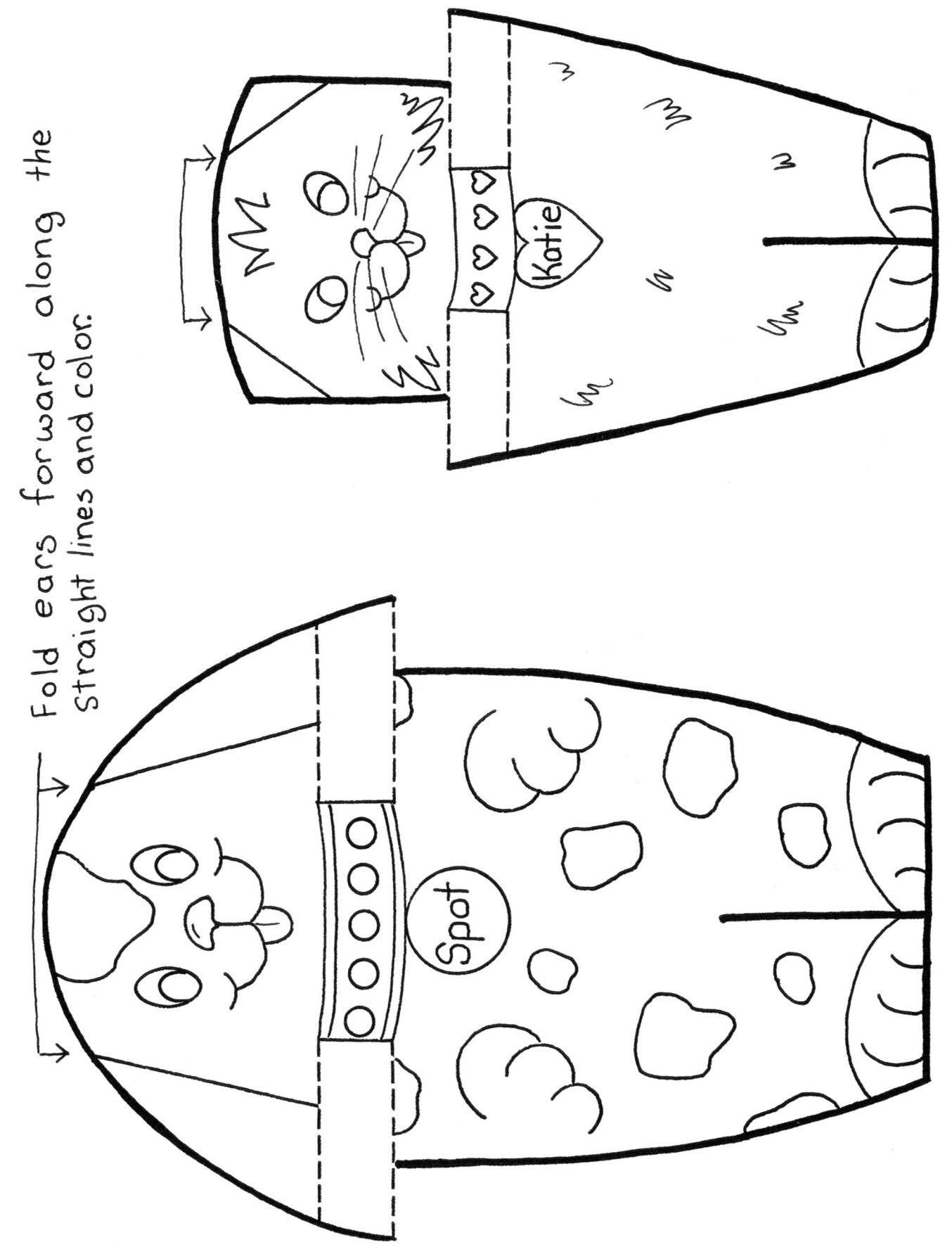

Fold ears forward along the straight lines and color.

© 1991 by Incentive Publications, Inc., Nashville, TN.

41

DINOSAUR DISPLAY

MATERIALS:
- construction paper
- crayons
- paste
- scissors

CONSTRUCTION:
1. Reproduce the patterns.
2. Color and cut out the patterns.
3. Paste tail to the dinosaur.
4. Fold pattern back along dotted lines. This will create a stand-up activity.
5. Paste dinosaur to the grass pattern.

USE:

Display the stand-up dinosaurs around the classroom.

Read *Dinosaurs Days* by Joyce Milton.

DINOSAUR PATTERN

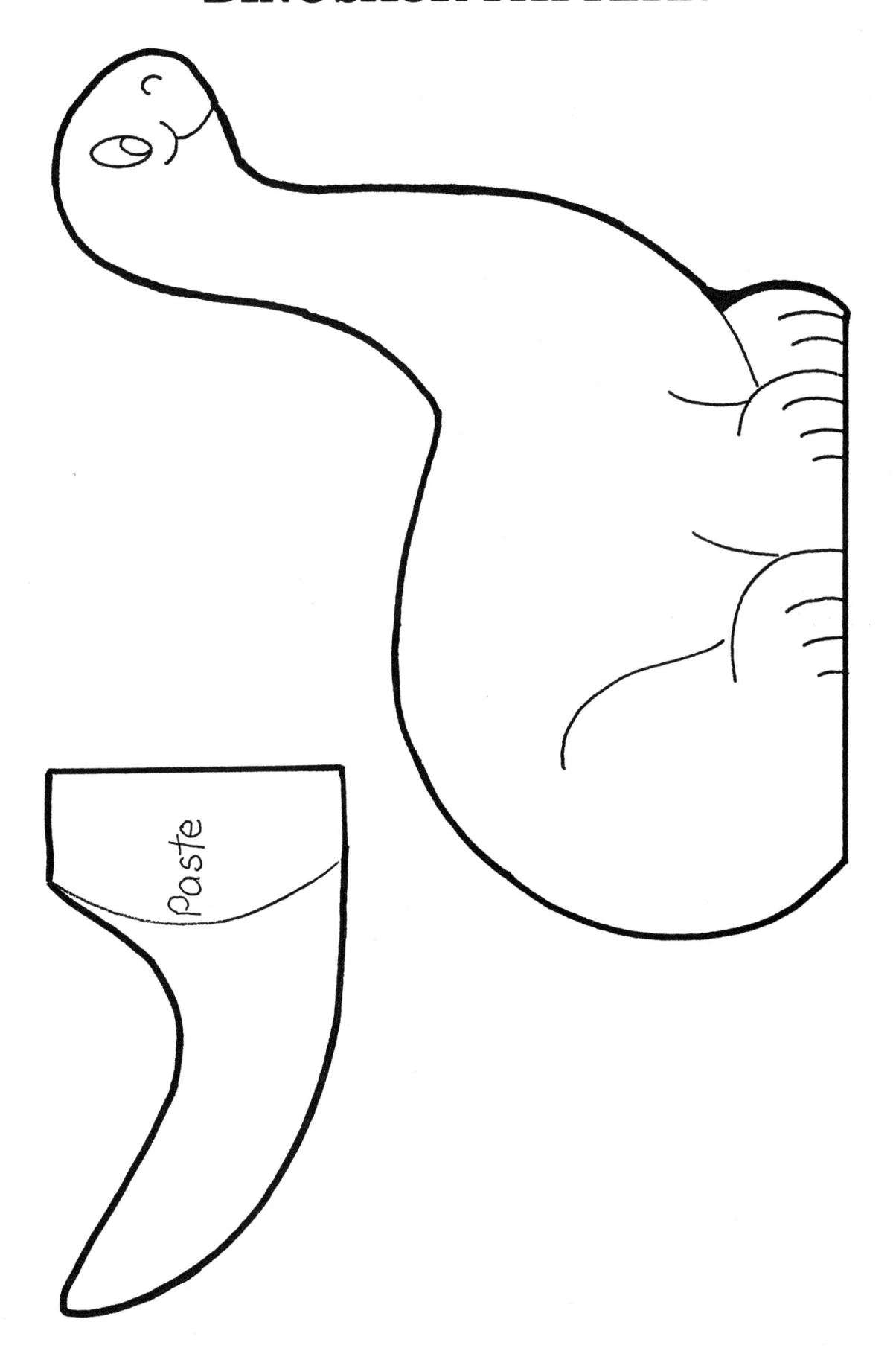

Paste

© 1991 by Incentive Publications, Inc., Nashville, TN.

GRASS PATTERN

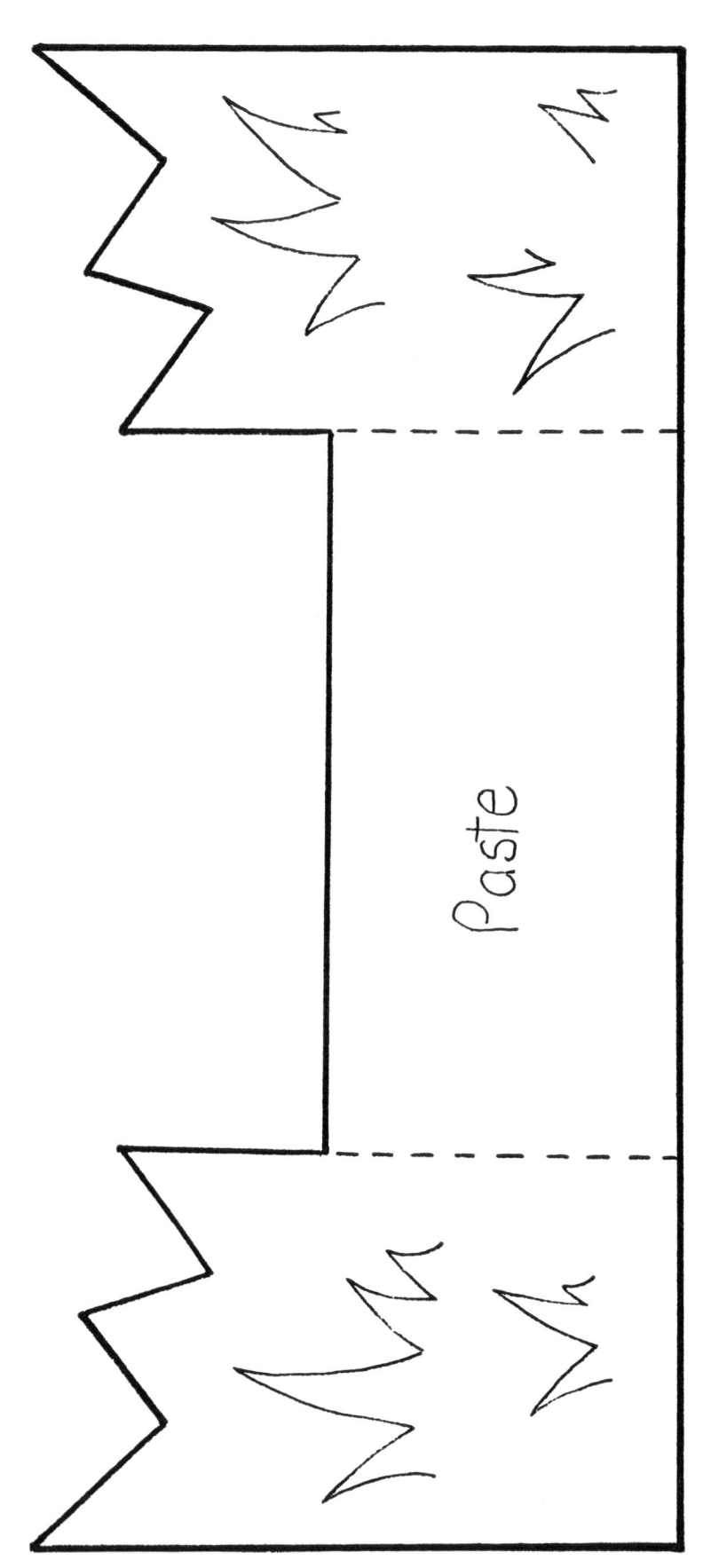

Paste

SAMMY SEAL BALANCES SHAPES

MATERIALS:
- construction paper
- crayons
- paste
- scissors

CONSTRUCTION:
1. Reproduce the shape patterns.
2. Have the students cut out the shapes and draw a funny face on each shape. Paste the four shapes to a 9" x 12" piece of construction paper.
3. Reproduce and cut out the seal patterns for the students.
4. Cut the patterns out of construction paper and/or color with crayons.
5. Reproduce the stand pattern and cut out. Fold a 9" x 12" piece of construction paper in half. Place the straight edge of the stand pattern on the fold of the paper. Trace the stand on construction paper, cut out, and decorate.
6. Attach the seal and stand to a bulletin board. Have the seal balancing the shapes. Display the students' shapes on the bulletin board.

USE:
This activity will aid in reinforcing shape recognition.

SEAL HEAD PATTERN

© 1991 by Incentive Publications, Inc., Nashville, TN.

SEAL TAIL PATTERN

SEAL STAND PATTERN

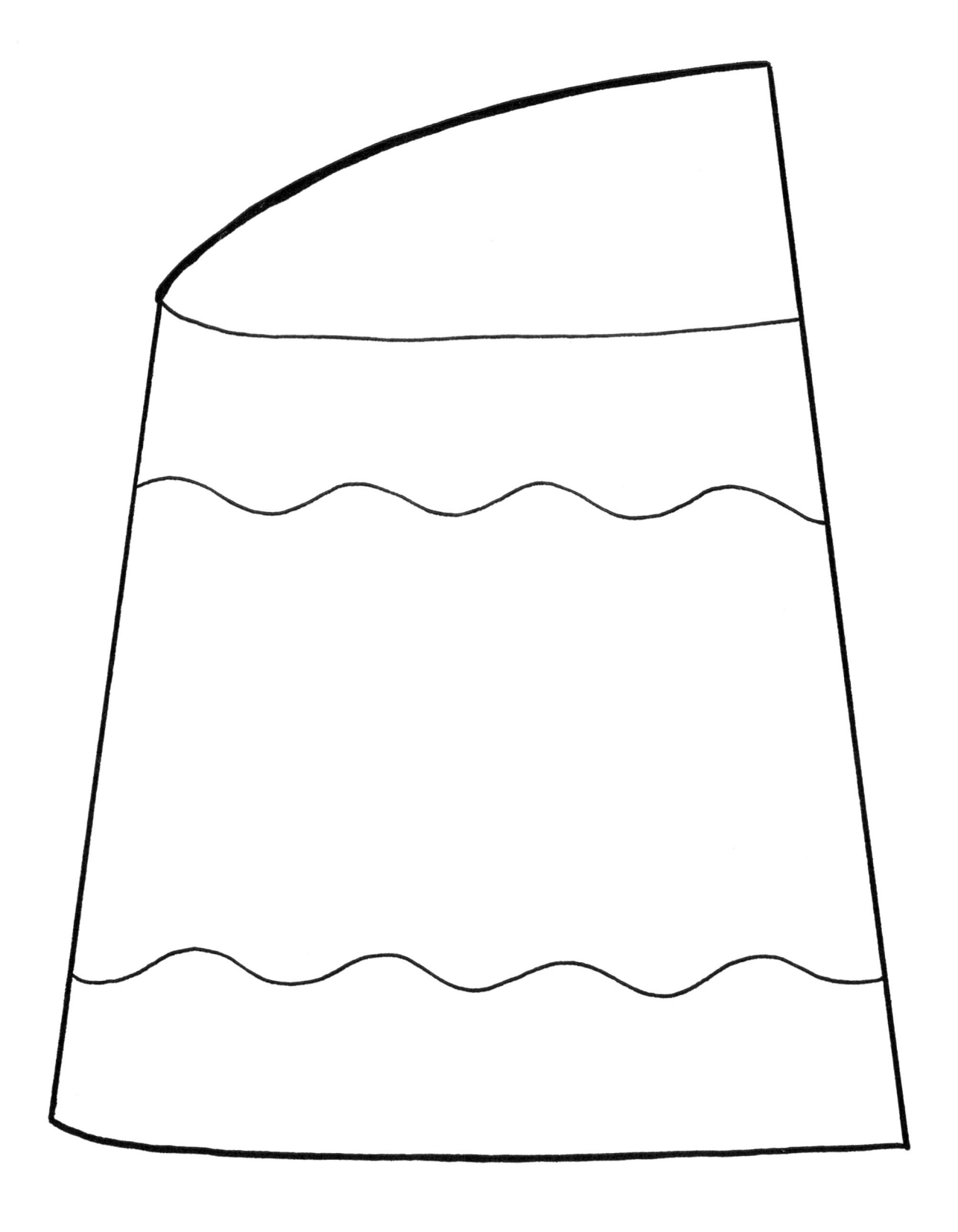

© 1991 by Incentive Publications, Inc., Nashville, TN.

SHAPE PATTERNS

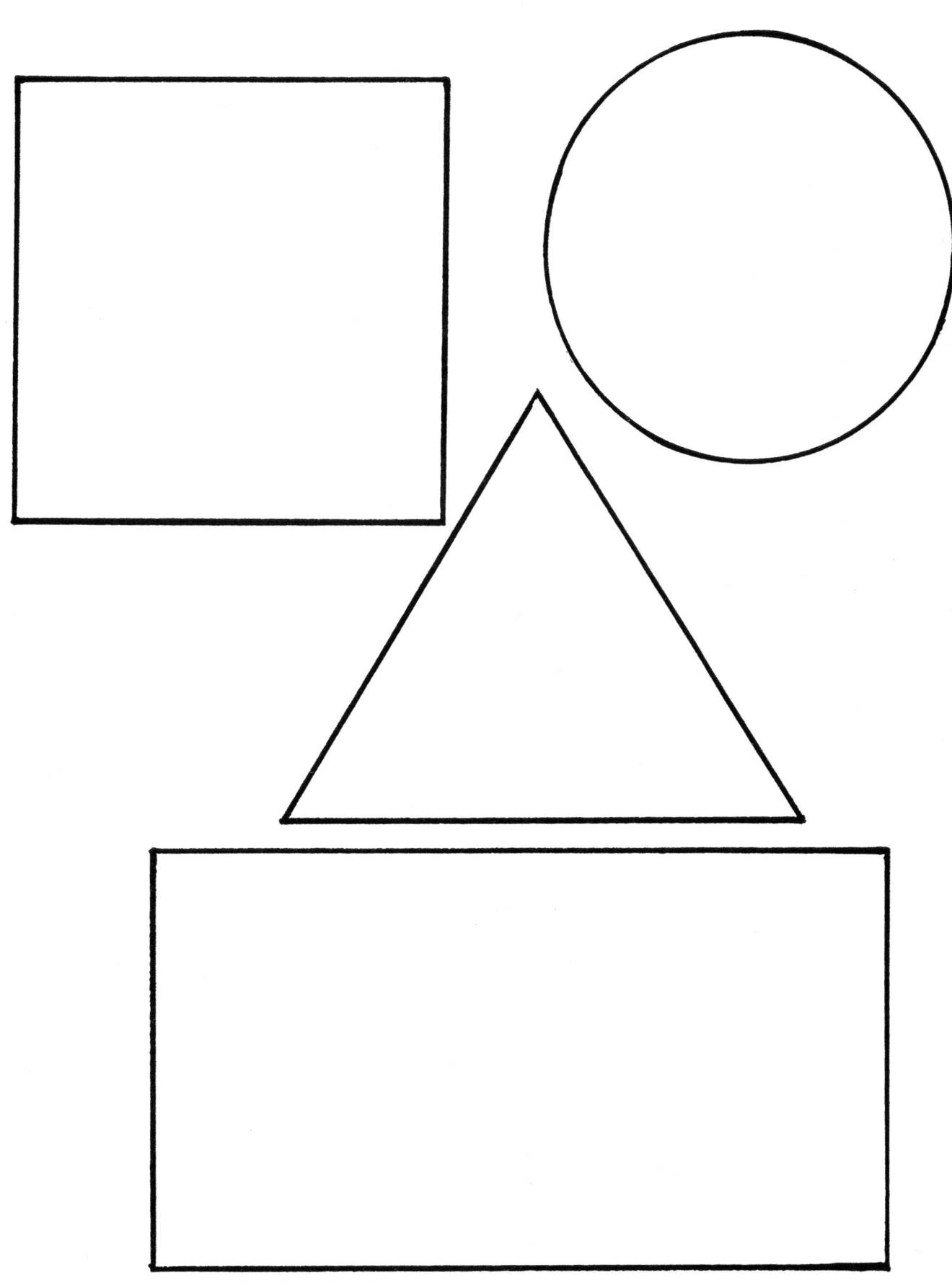

CERTIFICATES

MATERIALS:
- construction paper
- crayons
- scissors

CONSTRUCTION:
1. Reproduce and write the appropriate information on the certificates.
2. Color and cut out the certificates.

USE:
Let the students take home their certificates for display.

BEAR CERTIFICATE PATTERN

"Beary" Good Work

To:

From:

© 1991 by Incentive Publications, Inc., Nashville, TN.

CAT CERTIFICATE PATTERN

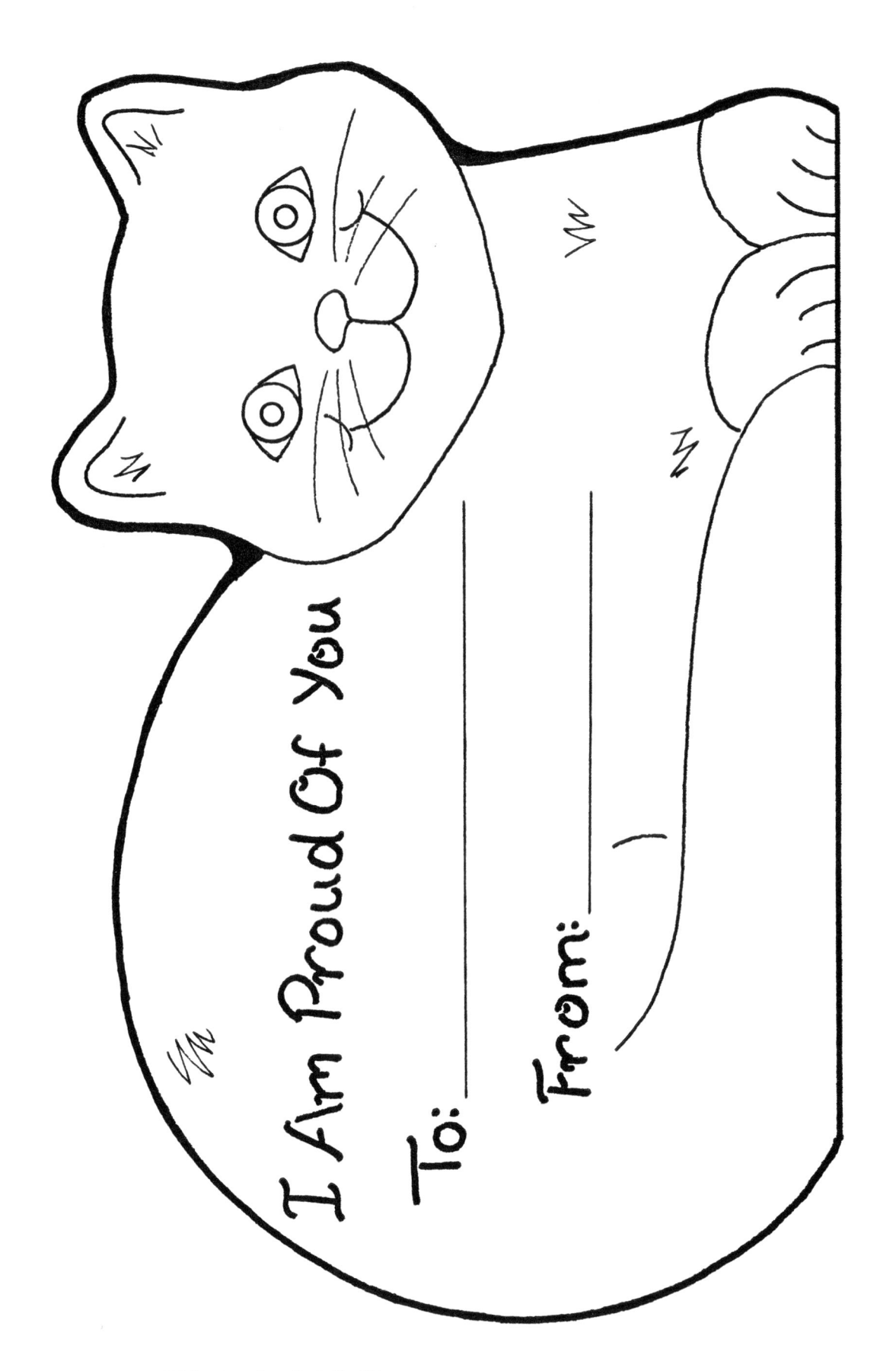

I Am Proud Of You

To: _____

From: _____

© 1991 by Incentive Publications, Inc., Nashville, TN.

DOG CERTIFICATE PATTERN

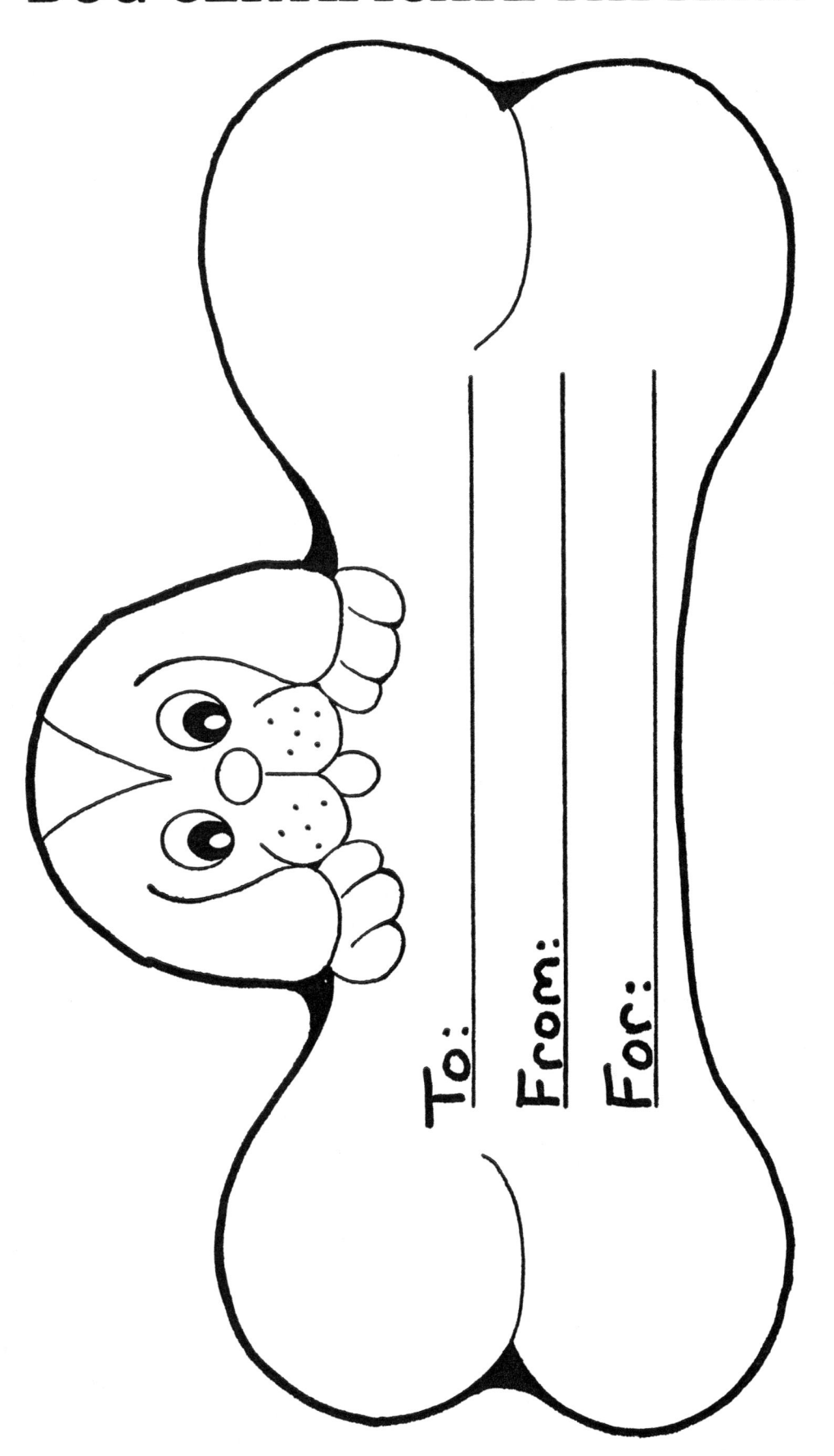

To:
From:
For:

© 1991 by Incentive Publications, Inc., Nashville, TN.

KITE CERTIFICATE PATTERN

Keep Up The Good Work

To: _____

From: _____

JACK-IN-THE-BOX

MATERIALS:
- construction paper
- crayons
- brads
- paste
- scissors

CONSTRUCTION:
1. Reproduce the patterns.
2. Color and cut out the patterns.
3. Insert a brad through the top part of the box and through the bottom part.
4. Write the appropriate information on the clown.
5. Fold the clown pattern like a fan along the lines.
6. Paste the clown to the box. Fold clown down, close the top, and then open the top and watch the clown pop out.

USE:

Reinforce numerals, colors, shapes, or new words with the jack-in-the-box.

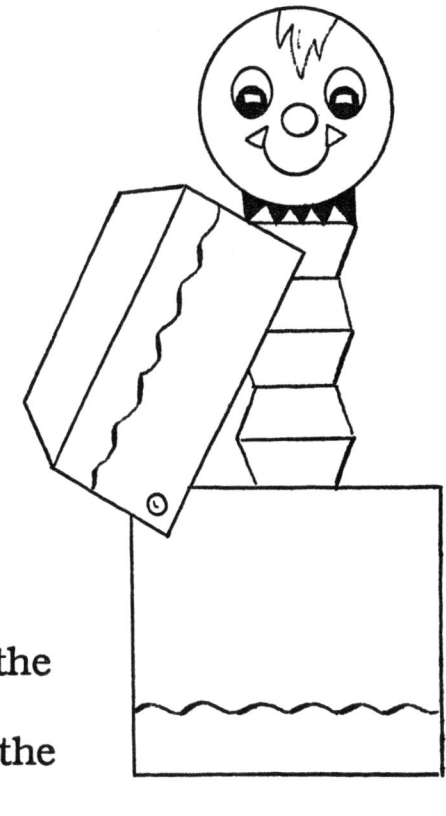

Back View

CLOWN PATTERN

1 one	numerals
red	colors
circle ○	shapes
ball	new words
	just for fun
Paste	

© 1991 by Incentive Publications, Inc., Nashville, TN.

STAND PATTERN

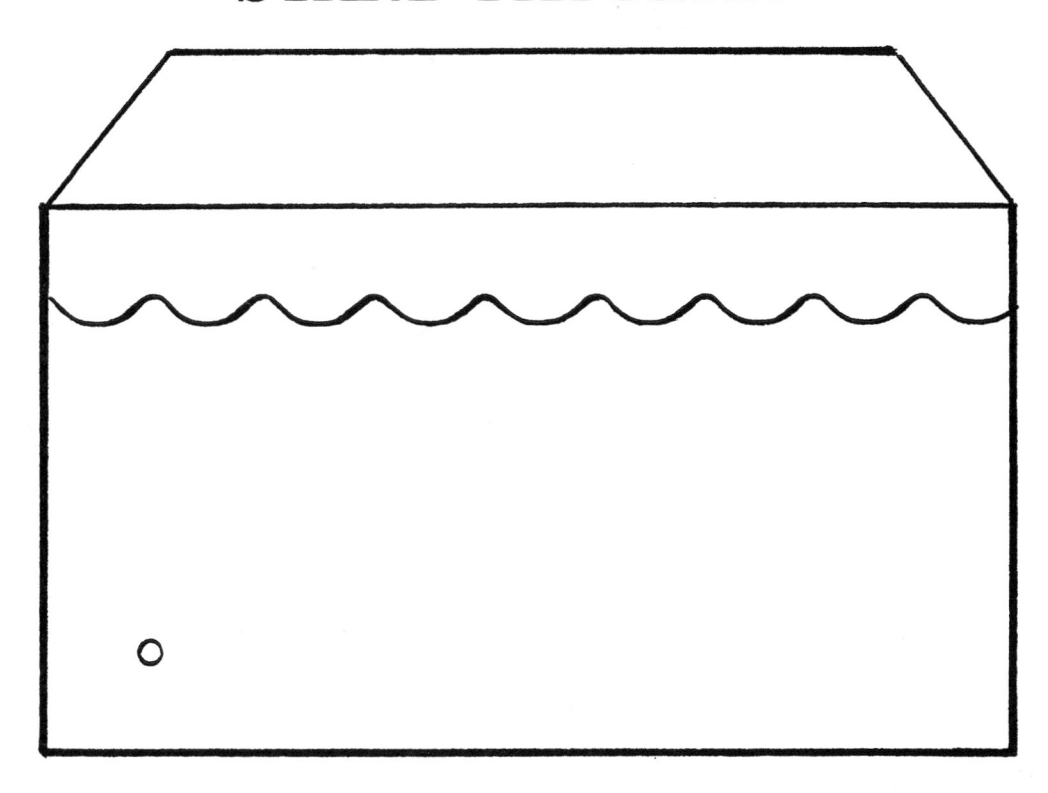

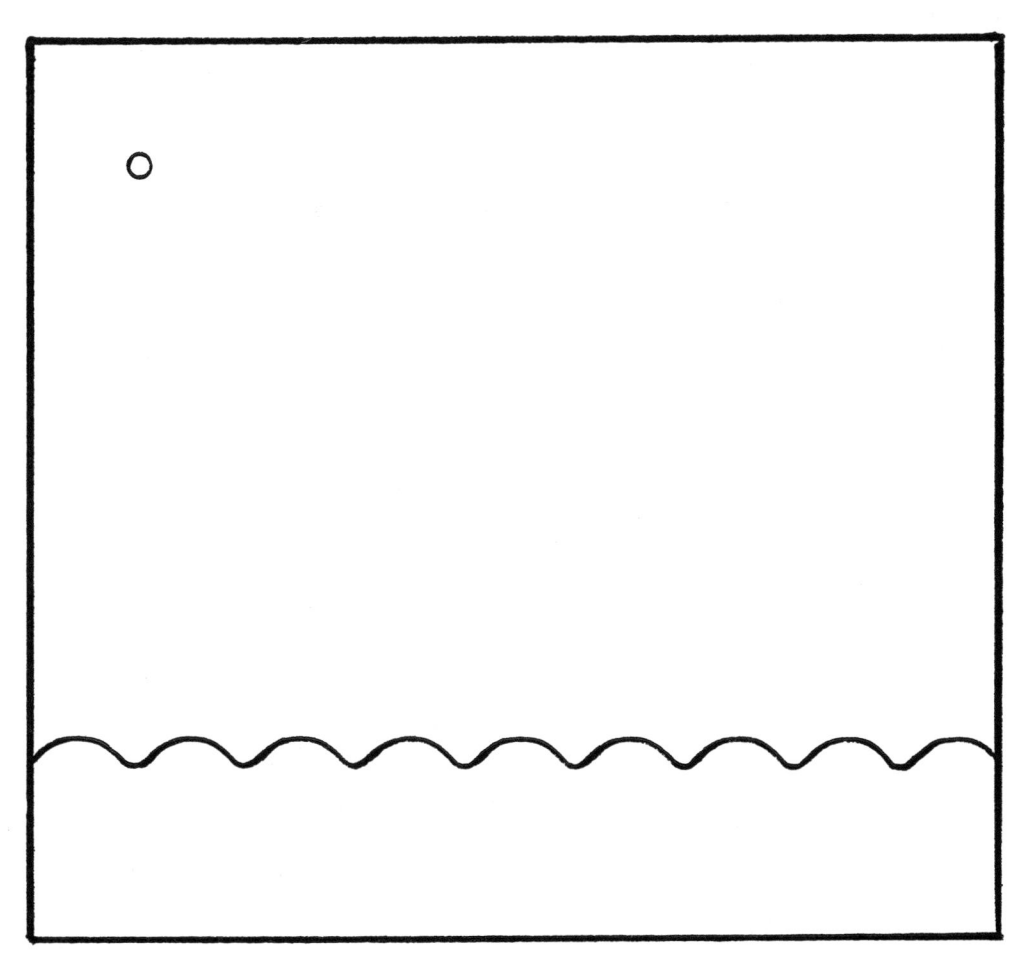

COLORED CRAYONS

MATERIALS:
- construction paper
- crayons
- paste
- scissors

CONSTRUCTION:
1. Reproduce the patterns.
2. Color and cut out the patterns.
3. Place a thin line of paste on each side of the crayon box. Fold the box in half and press the sides together.
4. Place the crayons in the box.

USE:
This activity will aid in teaching basic colors and color words.

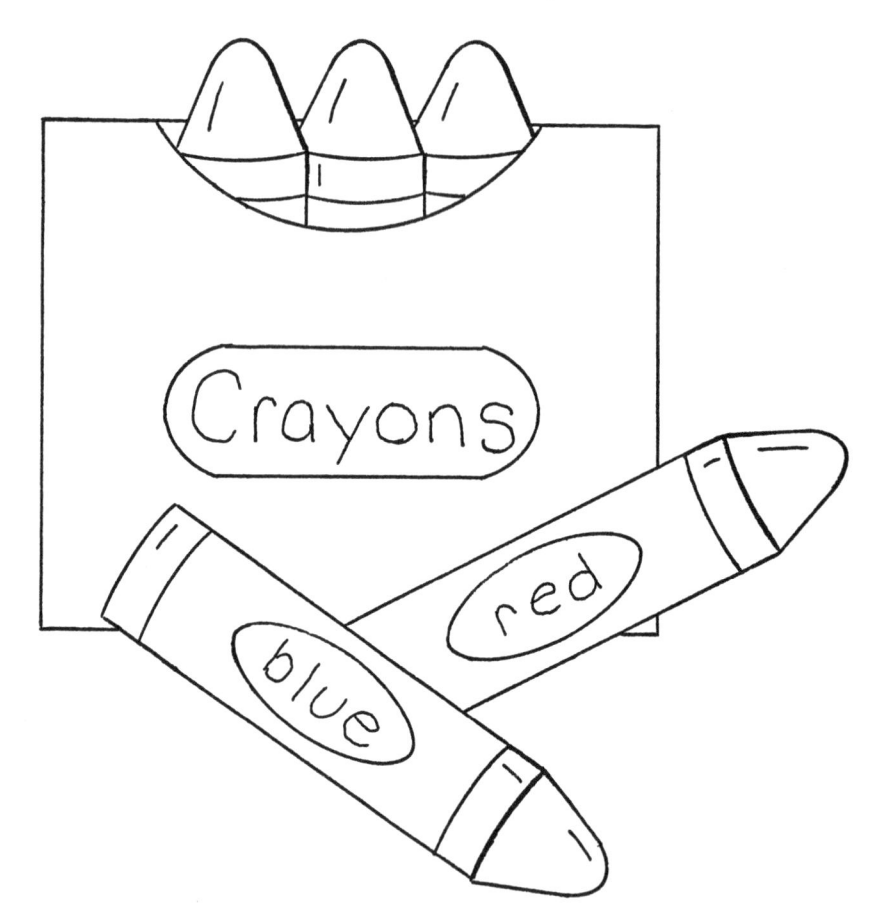

CRAYONS PATTERNS

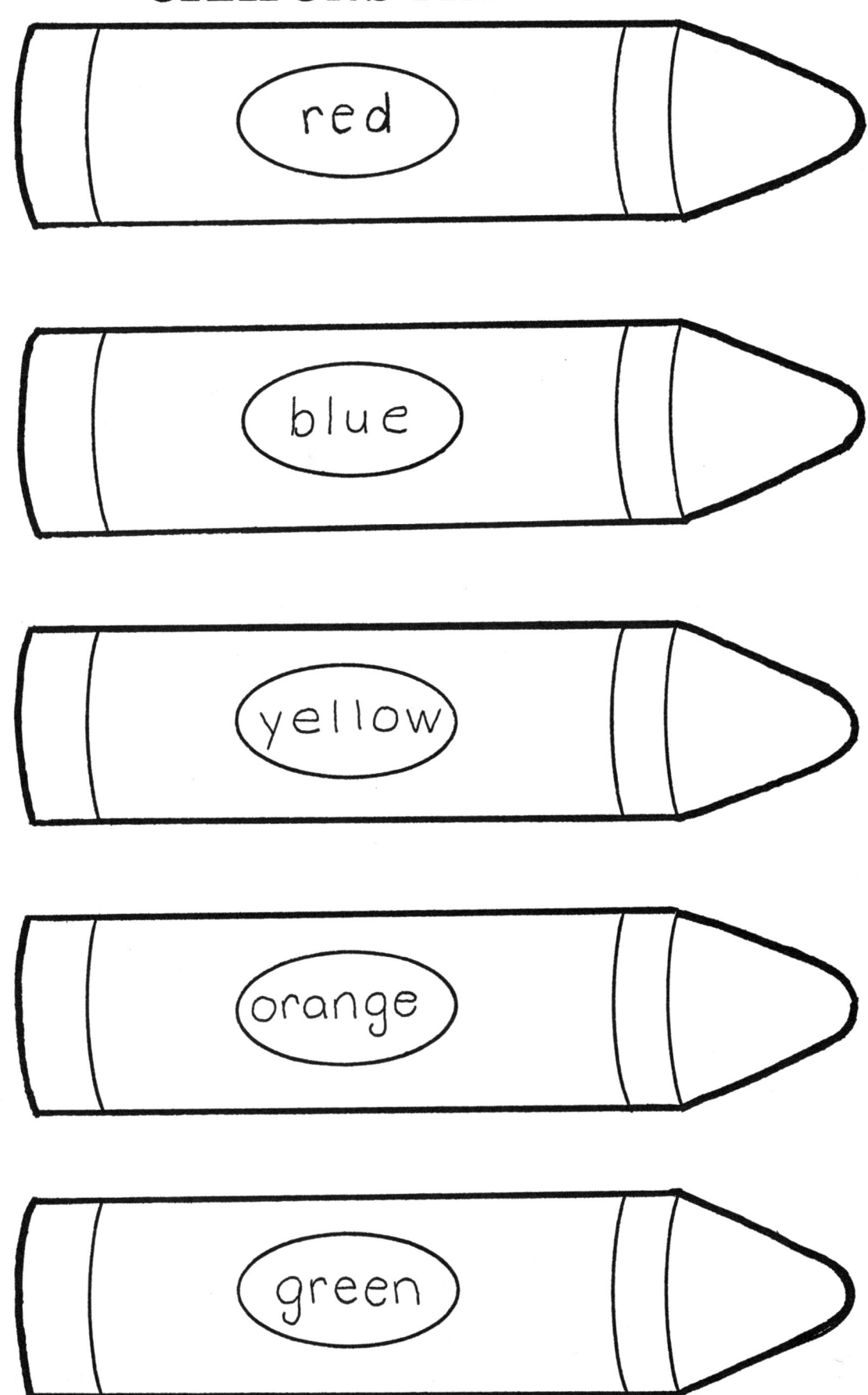

red

blue

yellow

orange

green

© 1991 by Incentive Publications, Inc., Nashville, TN.

CRAYON BOX PATTERN

GOOD DENTAL HABITS

MATERIALS:
- construction paper
- crayons
- scissors

CONSTRUCTION:
1. Reproduce the pattern.
2. Draw a face on the tooth and cut out.
3. Attach each student's tooth to a bulletin board.
4. Write good dental habits on construction paper and attach to the bulletin board.

USE:
The bulletin board will encourage good dental health habits.

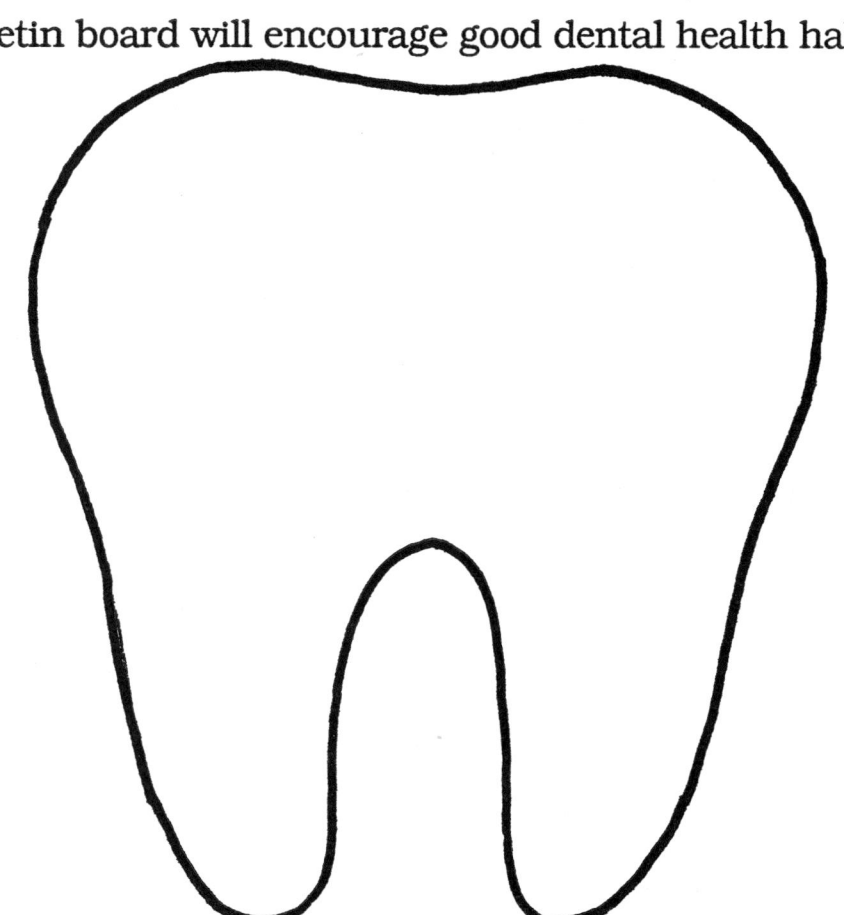

HELPER BEES

MATERIALS:
- construction paper
- crayons
- pipe cleaners
- paste
- scissors

CONSTRUCTION:
1. Reproduce the bee pattern.
2. Color and cut out the patterns.
3. Take a pipe cleaner and shape it into the bee's antenna. Place the antenna under the tab and paste.
4. Have the students write their names on the bees.
5. Reproduce the hive patterns and cut out for students. Fold a 9" x 12" piece of construction paper in half. Place the straight edge of the hive pattern on the fold of the paper. Trace the hive on yellow construction paper and cut out.
6. Write the classroom duties on the hive and attach to a bulletin board.
7. Attach a student's bee next to each duty. The classroom duty will be that student's responsibility for the day or for the week.
8. Reproduce the certificate; then write the student's name on it. Let the students color and cut out the certificates.

USE:
The bulletin board will aid in teaching classroom responsibilities. The students will enjoy receiving a certificate for being a good helper.

Read *Bees* Wonder Books

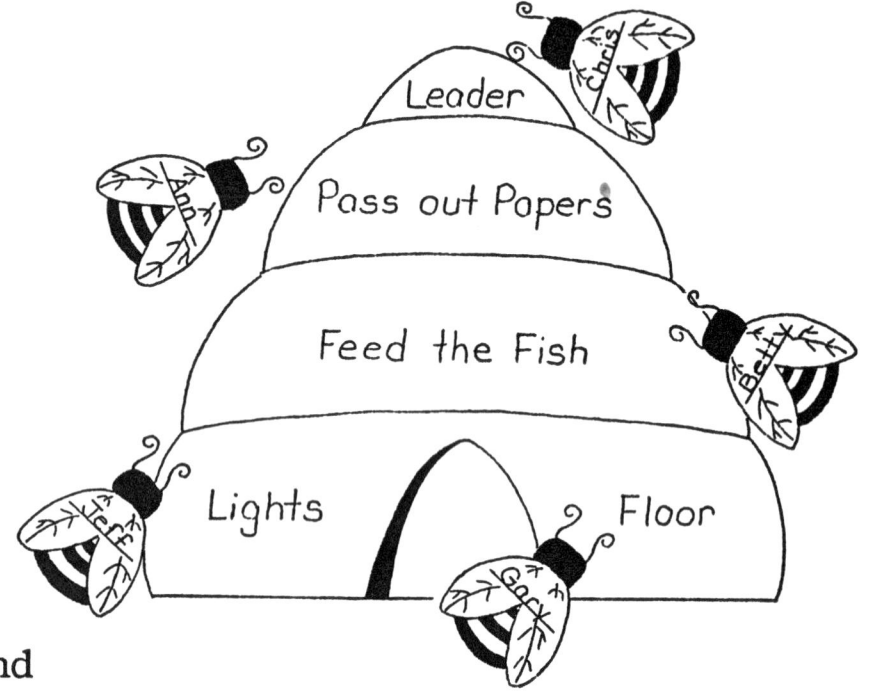

BEE PATTERN

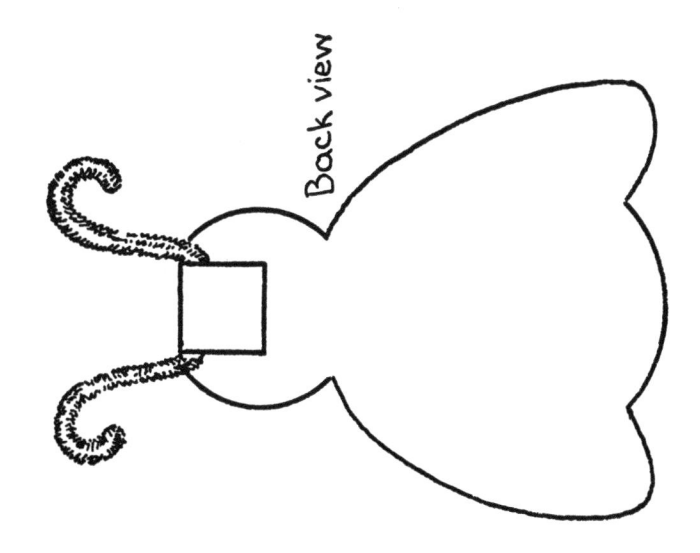

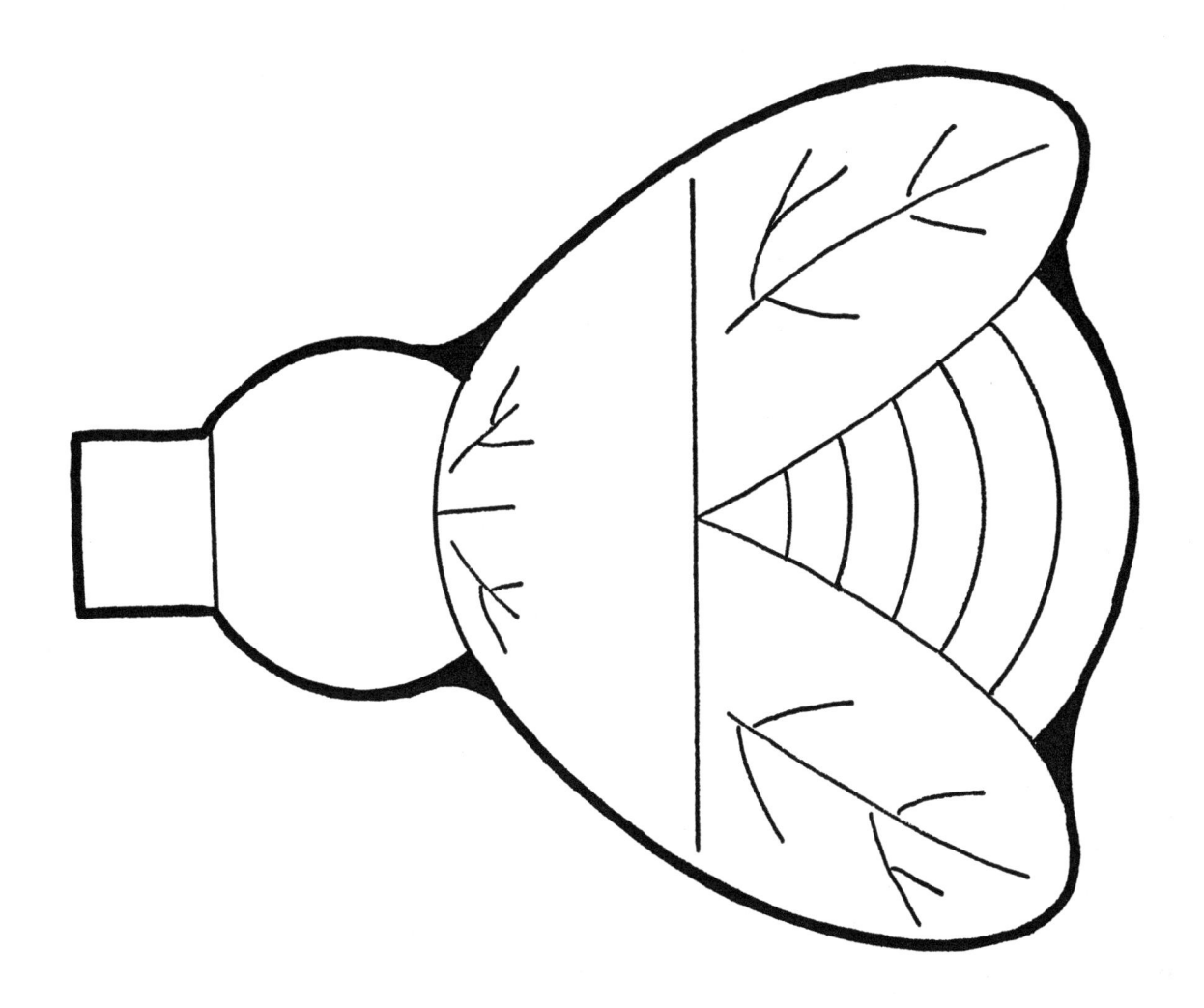

Back view

BEE HIVE PATTERN

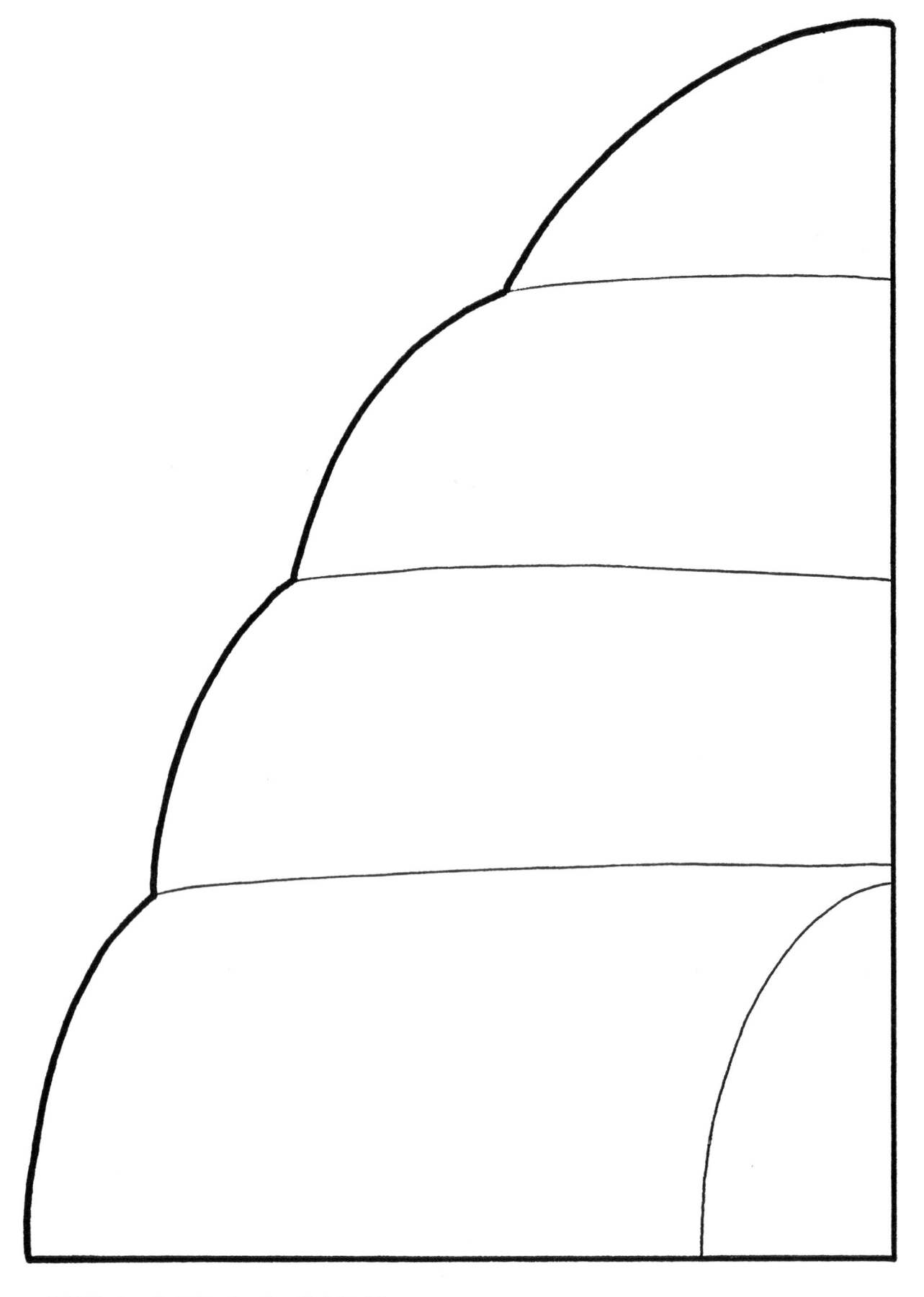

BEE HIVE CERTIFICATE

Thank You For Being A Good Helper

© 1991 by Incentive Publications, Inc., Nashville, TN.

HUMPTY-DUMPTY

MATERIALS:
- construction paper
- crayons
- paste
- scissors

CONSTRUCTION:
1. Reproduce the patterns.
2. Color and cut out the patterns. Let children fill in Humpty's facial features.
3. Paste Humpty-Dumpty to the wall.
4. Fold the wall pattern back along the dotted lines. This will form a stand-up wall.

USE:
Read the poem *Humpty-Dumpty* to the students; then let them make this activity to take home.

HUMPTY-DUMPTY

Humpty-Dumpty sat on a wall,
Humpty-Dumpty had a great fall.
All the King's horses and all the King's men,
Couldn't put Humpty together again.

© 1991 by Incentive Publications, Inc., Nashville, TN.

HUMPTY-DUMPTY WALL PATTERN

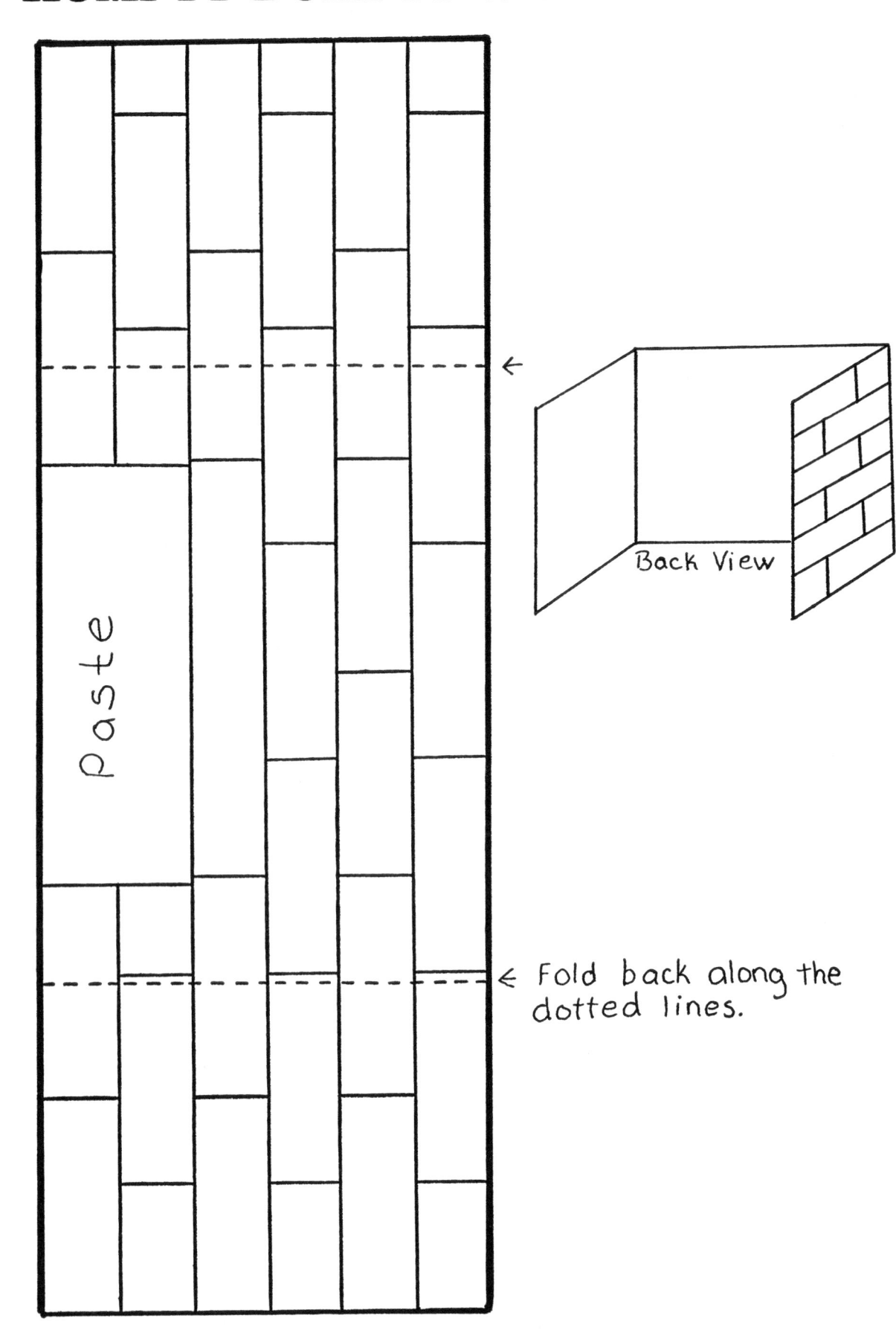

Paste

← Fold back along the dotted lines.

Back View

WEATHER BEAR

MATERIALS:
- construction paper
- brads
- crayons
- scissors

CONSTRUCTION:
1. Reproduce the patterns.
2. Color and cut out the patterns.
3. Insert a brad into the center of the wheel; then attach to the bear.
4. Turn the wheel to the appropriate weather section for the day. (Turn it to the bow tie.)

USE:

This activity will help students get interested in learning more about weather.

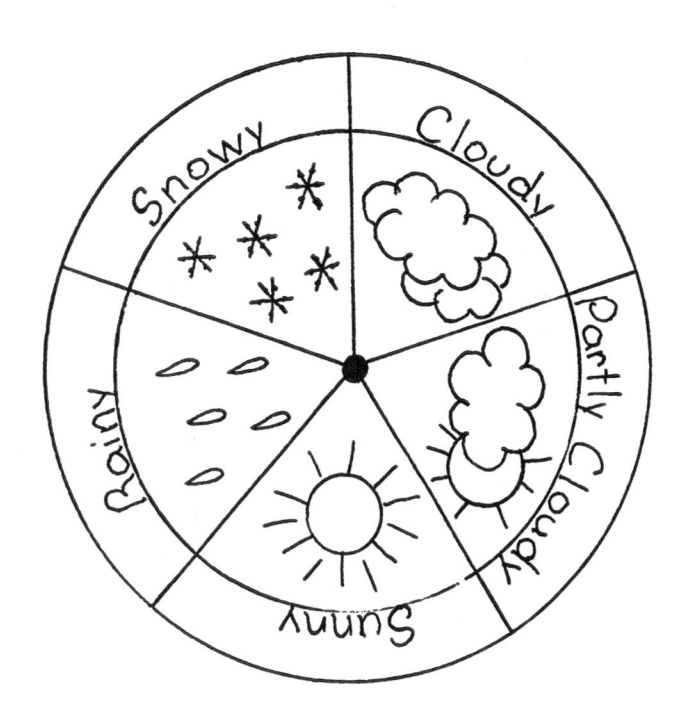

© 1991 by Incentive Publications, Inc., Nashville, TN.

BEAR PATTERN

© 1991 by Incentive Publications, Inc., Nashville, TN.

HAPPY HEN

MATERIALS:
- construction paper
- crayons
- paste
- scissors

CONSTRUCTION:
1. Reproduce the pattern.
2. Color and cut out the pattern.
3. Cut the nest along the dotted lines. Crumple the cut slits with your hands. This will add dimension to the nest.
4. Paste the hen to a piece of construction paper. (Do not place paste on the nest.)

USE:

This activity can be used when studying farm animals or after a hen story.

Read *The Little Red Hen*, Golden.

HEN PATTERN

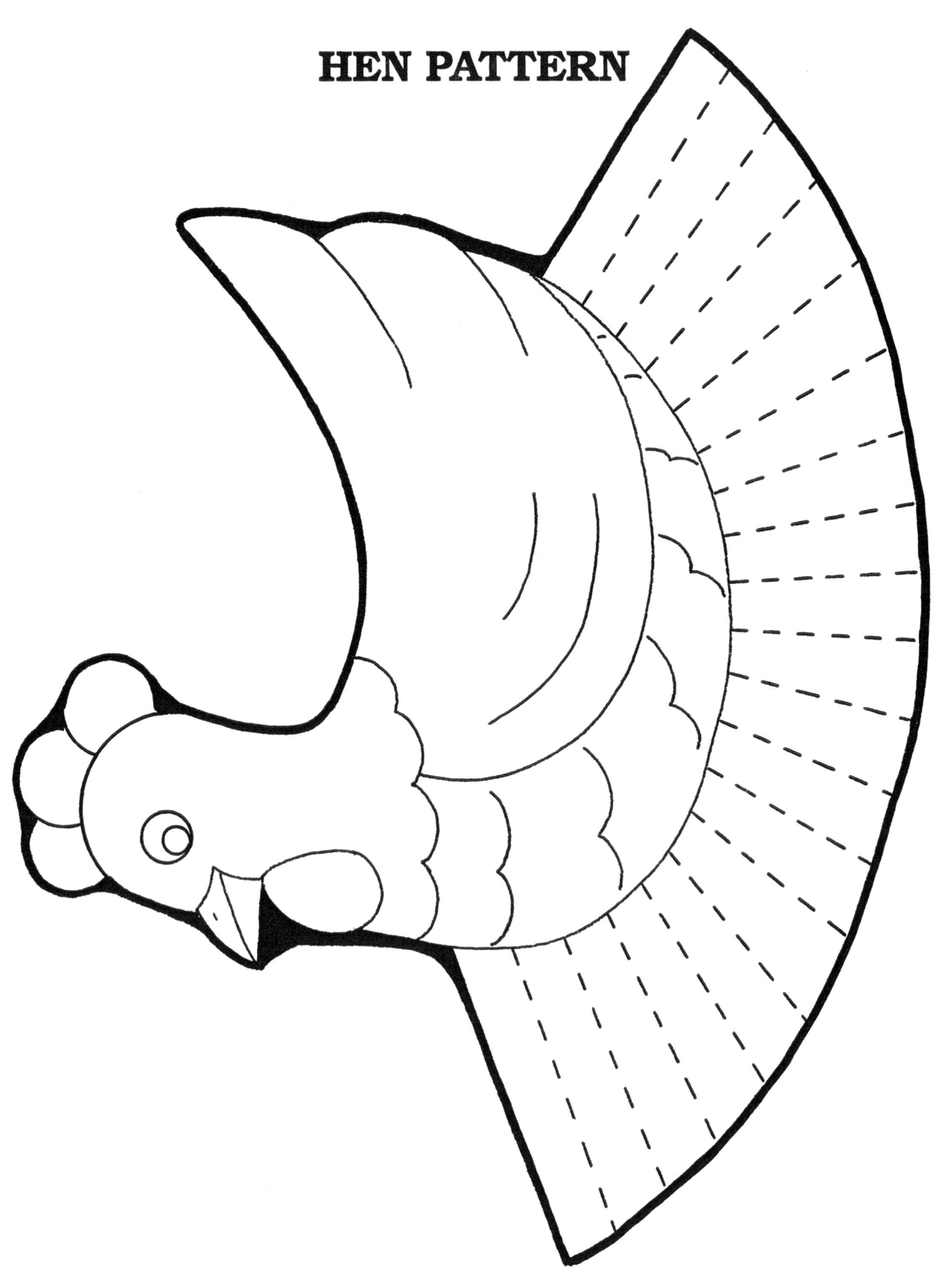

© 1991 by Incentive Publications, Inc., Nashville, TN.

ROARING GOOD TIME

MATERIALS:
- construction paper
- crayons
- paste
- scissors

CONSTRUCTION:
1. Reproduce the patterns.
2. Color and cut out the patterns.
3. Cut the lion's mane along the dotted lines. Crumple the cut slits with your hands. This will add dimension to the mane.
4. Paste the lion's head to the body; then paste the lion to the stand.
5. Have the students write their names on the stands.
6. Attach the lions to a bulletin board. Write "Ms. Smith's (teacher's name) Class Is Having A Roaring Good Time" as the heading on the bulletin board.

USE:

Use this bulletin board activity the first day of school. The students will enjoy seeing their lions displayed.

LION PATTERN

Paste

© 1991 by Incentive Publications, Inc., Nashville, TN.

LION STAND PATTERN

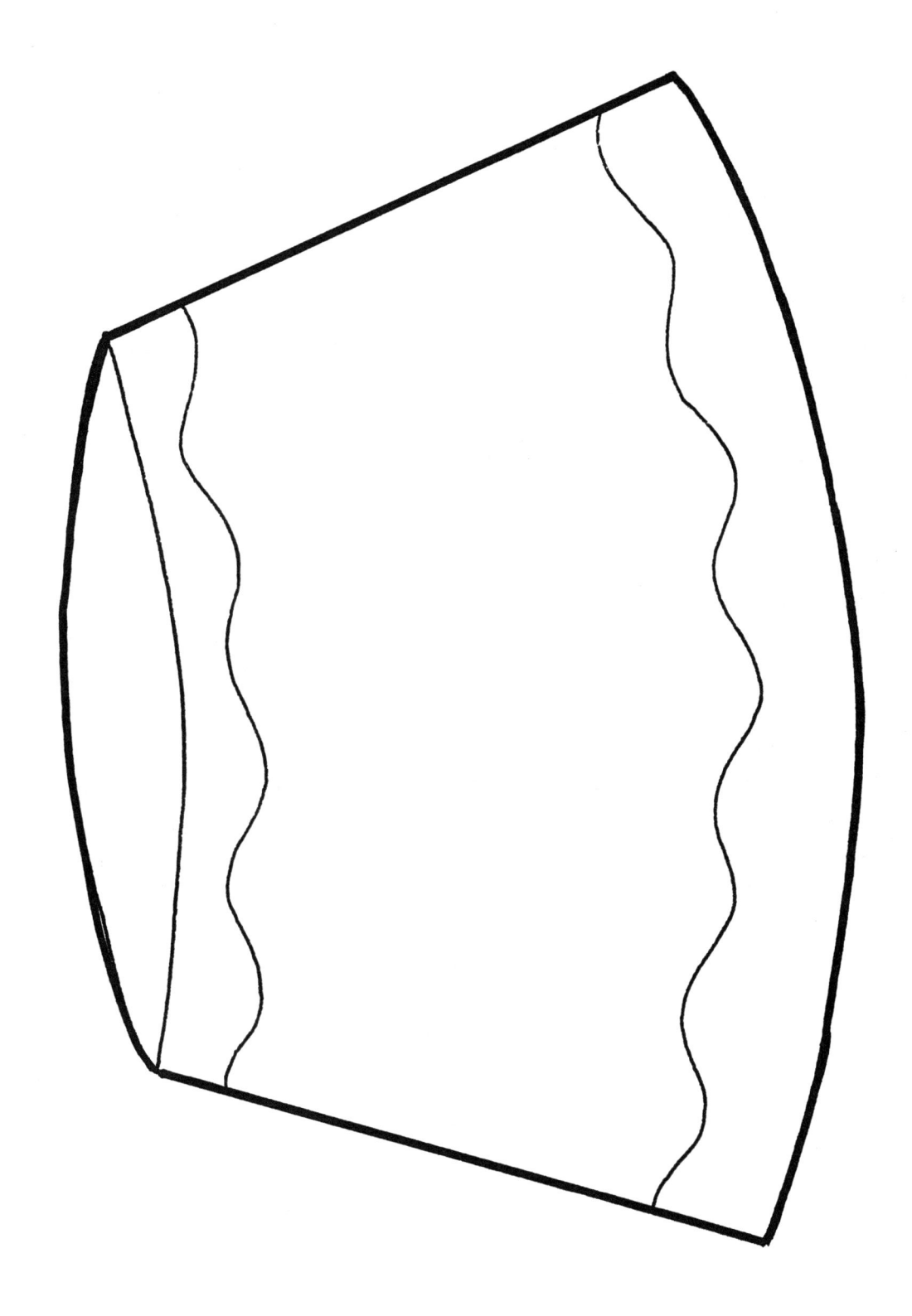

LADYBUG

MATERIALS:
- construction paper
- brads
- pipe cleaners
- crayons
- scissors

CONSTRUCTION:
1. Reproduce the patterns.
2. Color and cut out the patterns.
3. Insert a brad into the wings; then attach them to the ladybug. (The wings will open and close.)
4. Give each student a numeral to write on the ladybug. Instruct the students to draw dots on the wings to equal the numeral.

USE:
This activity will help reinforce counting skills and numeral recognition. Display the ladybugs on a bulletin board. Use the ladybugs for a learning center activity. (This is a self-check activity.)

LADYBUG PATTERN

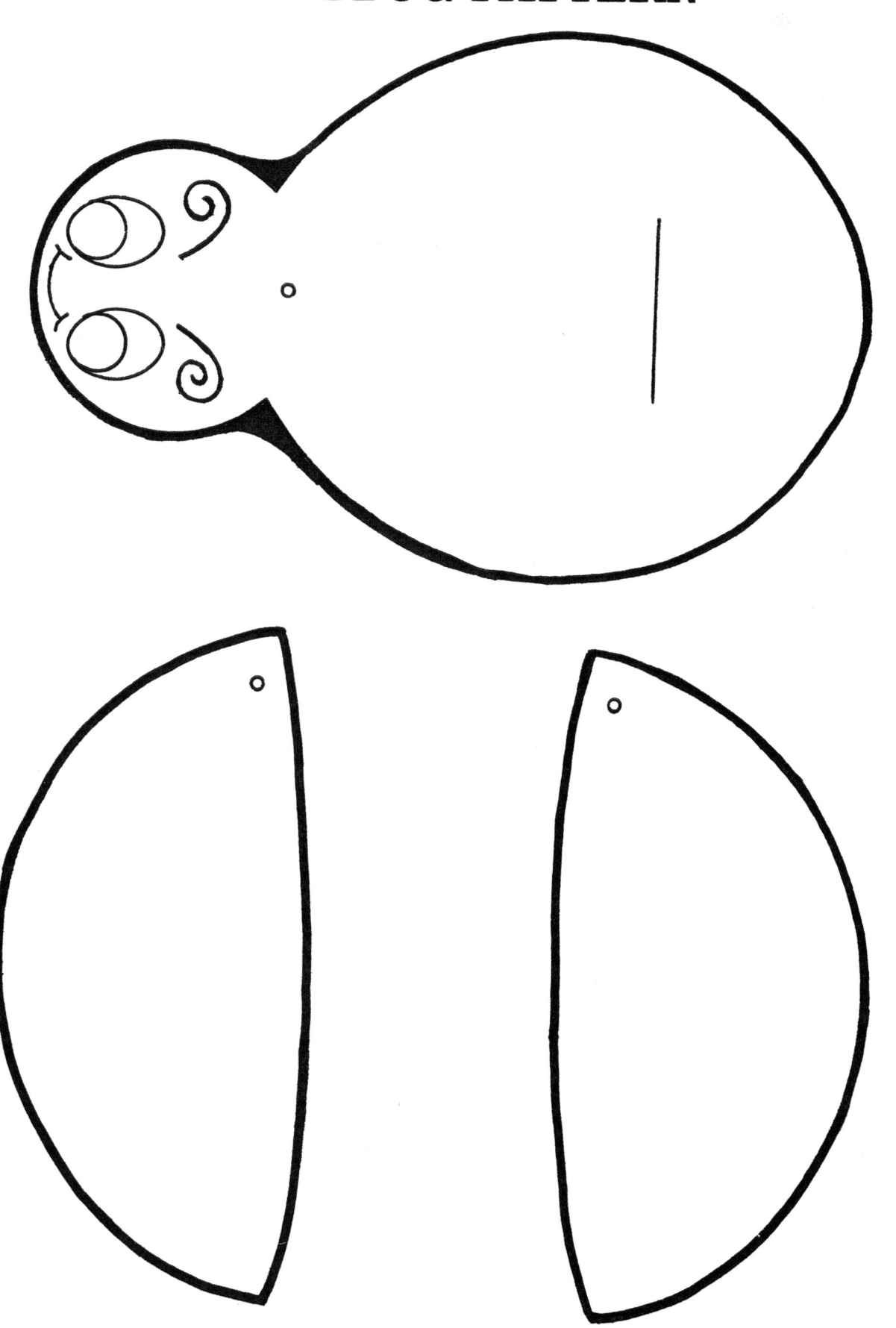

BEAUTIFUL BUTTERFLY

MATERIALS:
- construction paper
- crayons
- paste
- scissors

CONSTRUCTION:
1. Reproduce the patterns.
2. Color and cut out the patterns.
3. Fold the pattern in half along the dotted lines. Fold the wings back along the straight lines.
4. Paste the body of the butterfly to the wings.

USE:
The students will have fun playing with the butterflies. Attach yarn to the butterflies and display around the classroom. Use the butterflies as a springtime activity.

Read *Butterflies*, Wonder Books.

Fold in half.   Fold wings back.

BUTTERFLY PATTERN

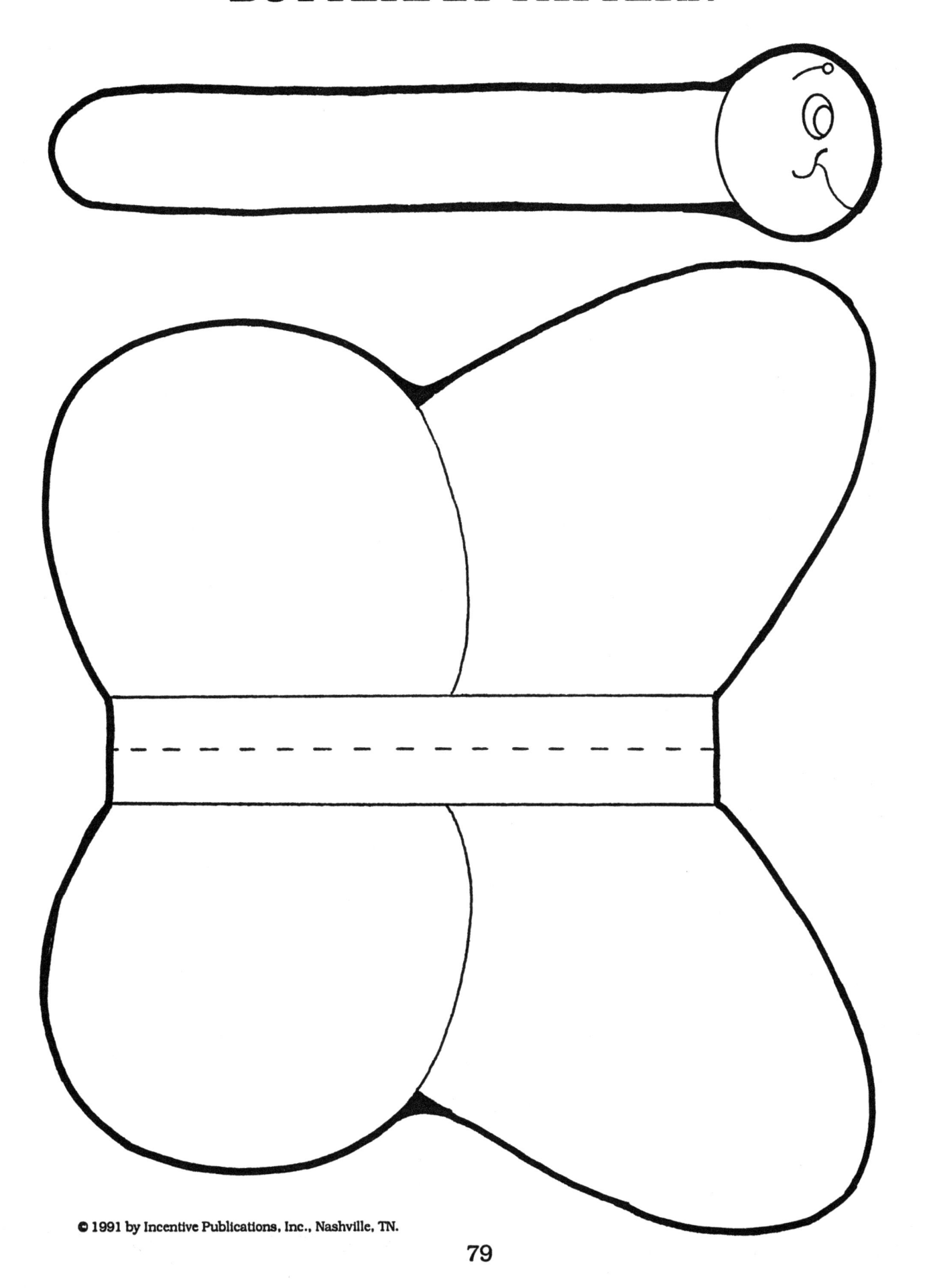

© 1991 by Incentive Publications, Inc., Nashville, TN.